STRATEGIES for Writers

Level A

Authors

Leslie W. Crawford, Ed.D.
Georgia College & State University

Rebecca Bowers Sipe, Ed.D.
Eastern Michigan University

Robert C. Calfee, Ph.D.
University of California, Riverside

Zaner-Bloser

Educational Consultants

Barbara Marinak
Reading Supervisor
Mechanicsburg, PA

Barry Sneed
Master Primary Teacher
Perry, OH

Catherine C. Thome, Ed.D.
English/Language Arts and Assessment Coordinator
Educational Services Division
Lake County Regional Office of Education
Grayslake, IL

Teacher Reviewers

Janice Andrus, Chanhassen, MN
Shannon Basner, Hollis, NY
Teressa D. Bell, Nashville, TN
Eve Bilbrey, Nashville, TN
Victoria B. Casady, Ferguson, MO
Kristin Cashman, Mechanicsburg, PA
Jeanie Denaro, Brooklyn, NY
Susan Friedman, Ph.D., Sharon, PA
Katherine Harrington, Mechanicsburg, PA
Dianna L. Hinderer, Ypsilanti, MI

Eleanor Kane, Stow, OH
Jean Kochevar, Minneapolis, MN
Diane L. Nicholson, Pittsburgh, PA
Susan Peery, San Antonio, TX
David Philpot, San Francisco, CA
Jodi Ramos, San Antonio, TX
Jacqueline Sullivan, Sunnyvale, CA
Rita Warden-Short, Brentwood, TN
Emily Williams, Nashville, TN
Roberta M. Wykoff, Stow, OH

Page Design Concepts and Cover Design

Tommaso Design Group

Photo Credits

Models: George C. Anderson Photography

Art Credits

Dave Aikins

Production by Marilyn Rodgers Bahney Paselsky

ISBN 0-7367-1837-0

Table of Contents

Writing and Writing Process Readiness

Table of Contents

NARRATIVE
Writing to Tell a Story

Table of Contents

DESCRIPTIVE
Writing to Describe

EXPOSITORY
Writing to Give Information

Table of Contents

PERSUASIVE
Writing to Tell What I Think

Writing and **Writing Process**
Readiness

Use this readiness section with the *Strategies for Writers* Big Books to introduce the four
writing modes and to develop writing readiness and writing process readiness.
Later, make student-sized versions of these same Big Books
(included in the Student Edition) to use during the writing process.

Student-Sized
Narrative Big Book,
My Big Day!

Student-Sized
Descriptive Big Book,
What Do We Have?

Student-Sized
Expository Big Book,
Show and Tell

Student-Sized
Persuasive Big Book,
I Love Oranges!

Writing Readiness:
The Alphabet

Connect the Dots

Name

To the Teacher: Review the letters of the alphabet by having children sing the "Alphabet Song." Tell children they are going to connect the dots to complete a picture. Have children start at the star and move from A to Z. Recite the letters with the children as they complete the picture. See "Sound-Symbol Awareness" on page T9C for information on how to use the write-on line. More activities are in the Teacher Edition.

Writing Readiness:
Capital and Lowercase Letters

Help the Bus Find the School

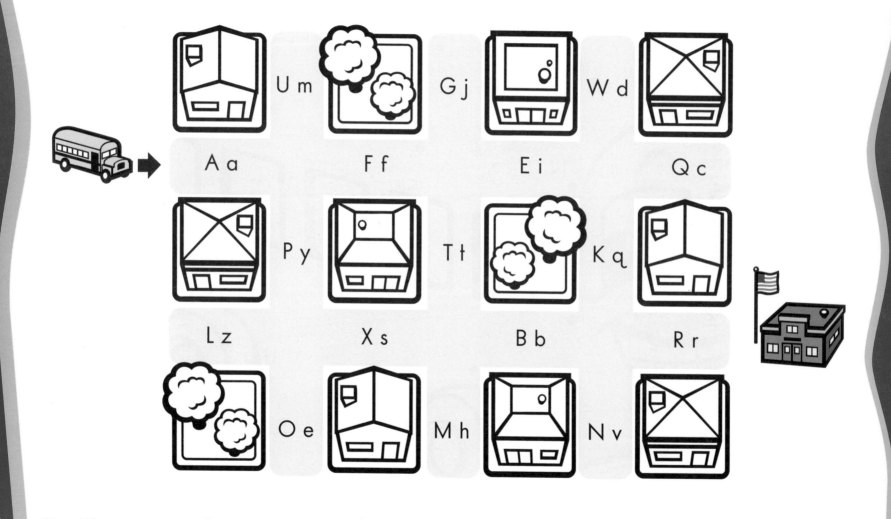

U m G j W d

A a F f E i Q c

P y T t K q

L z X s B b R r

O e M h N v

Name

Ms. Smith

A
B
C

cat

January

To the Teacher: Have children study the picture. Then ask them to identify a variety of objects on the left, right, top, and bottom of the picture. You may wish to use the suggested directions on page TIIA in the Teacher Edition. See the Teacher Edition for more activities.

11

Search the Cubby

To the Teacher: This activity prepares the child to gather information. Explain that this is Yan's cubby. Have children name and describe the items they see in her cubby. Have them decide which things Yan will need to take or "gather" from the cubby (l.) for class; (2.) for recess; (3.) for a field trip. Have children color the "class" items red, the "recess" items blue, and the "field trip" items green. It is not essential that all agree with the choices so long as good reasons are given. See the Teacher Edition for more activities.

Tell What's Next

Name

To the Teacher: This activity prepares the child to organize information to make a storyboard. Have children discuss the pictures of Yan at the top of the page. Ask them to write 1, 2, or 3, under each picture to show what happened first, next, and last. Then have them study the pictures below. Explain that these pictures tell a story and that the things that happen in stories are usually told in the order in which they happen. Have children decide what the third picture should be and draw it in the red box. See the Teacher Edition for more activities.

13

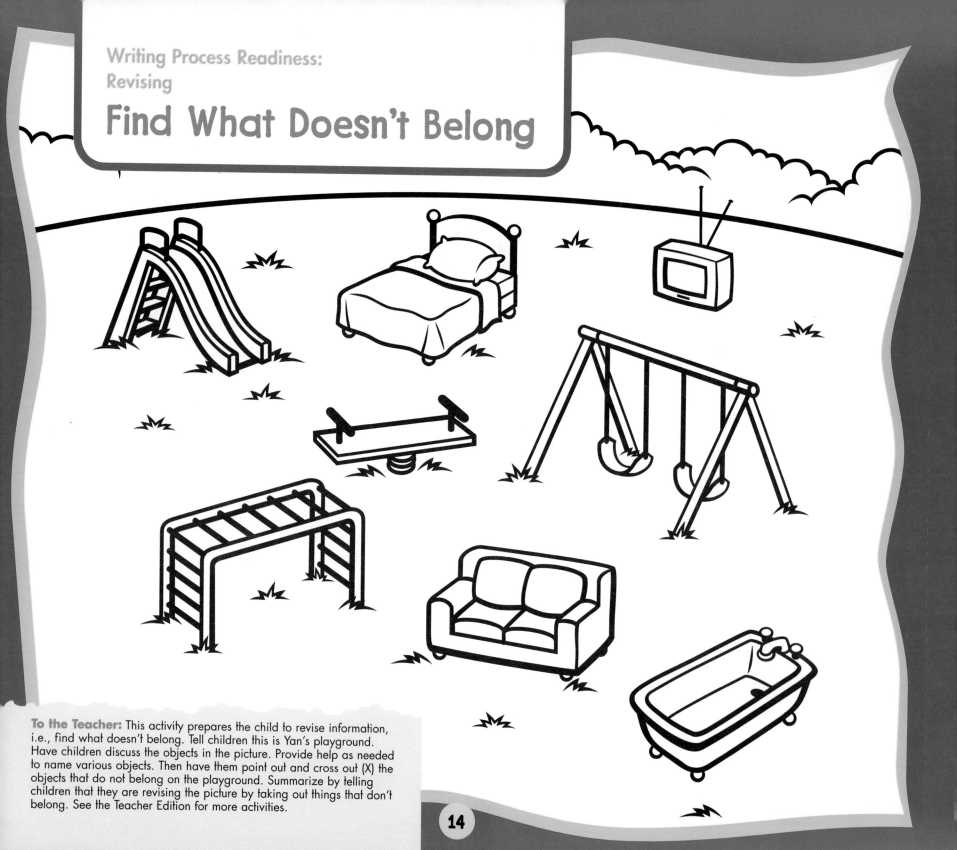

Find What Doesn't Belong

To the Teacher: This activity prepares the child to revise information, i.e., find what doesn't belong. Tell children this is Yan's playground. Have children discuss the objects in the picture. Provide help as needed to name various objects. Then have them point out and cross out (X) the objects that do not belong on the playground. Summarize by telling children that they are revising the picture by taking out things that don't belong. See the Teacher Edition for more activities.

14

Find the Letter

Name

1. p   b   c

2. n   f   m

3. p   r   d

4. s   v   t

5. p   h   k

6. j   g   l

To the Teacher: Guide children to name the toys in the top row: *ball, net, duck*. As each item is named, say the word, emphasizing the initial consonant sound. Have children circle the letter that stands for that initial sound. Then guide children to name the toys in the bottom row: *boat, top, dog*. As each item is named, say the word, emphasizing the ending sound. Have children circle the letter that stands for that ending sound. For oral language development, have children say words that rhyme with the name of each picture. Ask children to write the name of another toy on the write-on line at the bottom of the page. (Accept developmental spelling.) See the Teacher Edition for more activities.

Write the Lowercase Letter

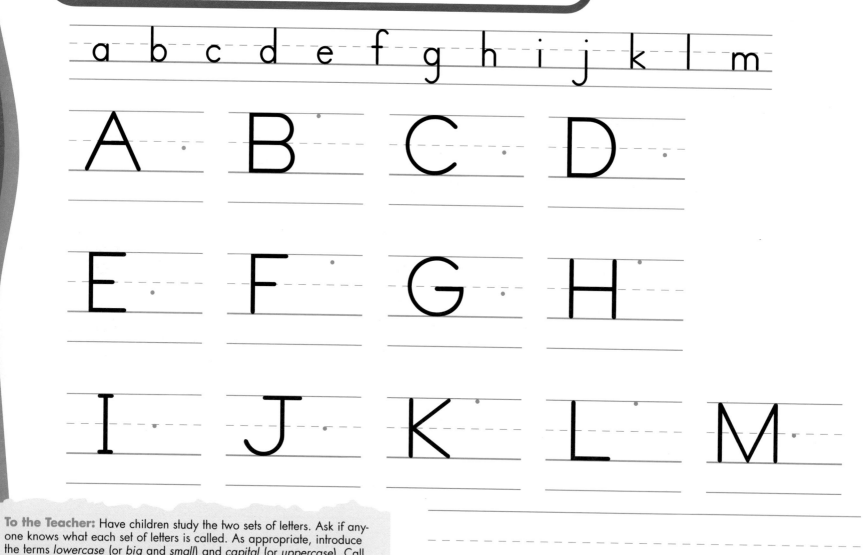

a b c d e f g h i j k l m

A B C D

E F G H

I J K L M

To the Teacher: Have children study the two sets of letters. Ask if any-one knows what each set of letters is called. As appropriate, introduce the terms *lowercase* (or *big* and *small*) and *capital* (or *uppercase*). Call attention to the first capital letter and ask children to identify the letter (i.e., capital A). Then have them find the small *a* in the first line and write it next to its capital form. Have children start at the dot. Repeat the process with several letters until children are able to proceed on their own. Ask children to write words on the write-on lines at the bottom of the pages. (Accept developmental spelling.) See the Teacher Edition for more activities.

n o p q r s t u v w x y z

N O P Q

R S T U

V W X Y Z

Describe the Picture

1. airplane
2. boat
3. wings
4. windows
5. red and white
6. blue and yellow

Tell About It

Name _____

Both

To the Teacher: This activity prepares the child to organize information to make a Venn diagram. Explain the Venn's use in comparing and contrasting two things. Ask children to identify the pictures in the Venn. Guide them in writing *skates* and *bike* under the appropriate picture. Ask children a series of questions about the skates, bike, or both. "Which one do you sit on?" (bike) Write the word *sit* on the board and have children copy it in the blue circle. Repeat the process with the questions on page T19 in the Teacher Edition. On the write-on line at the bottom of the page, ask children to write another word that describes the skates or the bike or both. (Accept developmental spelling.) See the Teacher Edition for more activities.

Add the Missing Parts

Write the Words

Name

1. my <u>dog</u> on a _____

2. a <u>man</u> by the _____

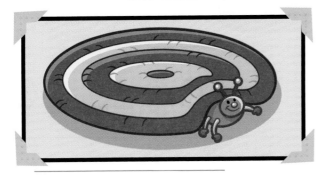

3. a _____ under the <u>rug</u>

4. a _____ in a <u>pen</u>

To the Teacher: Explain that Brad started to label each picture he took of things around his house, but he didn't finish the job. Tell children they will finish the labels by adding missing words. Call attention to the first picture, and ask children what this picture shows. Repeat "my dog on a log" several times, then have children add the missing word. Point out that each word they write will rhyme with the underlined word. Repeat the process with the remaining pictures. See the Teacher Edition for more activities.

Writing Readiness:
Making Words With Clusters

Listen and Learn

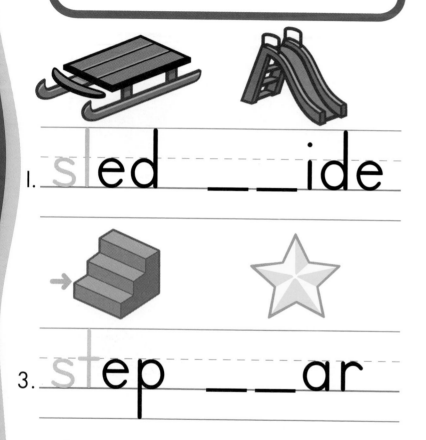

1. s̲l̲ed ___ide

2. f̲r̲og ___ame

3. s̲t̲ep ___ar

4. d̲r̲um ___ess

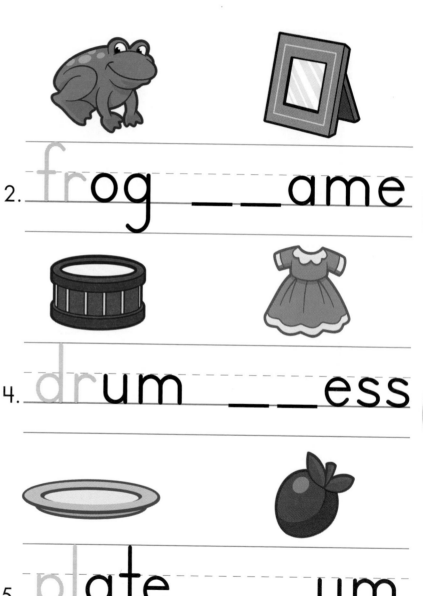

5. p̲l̲ate ___um

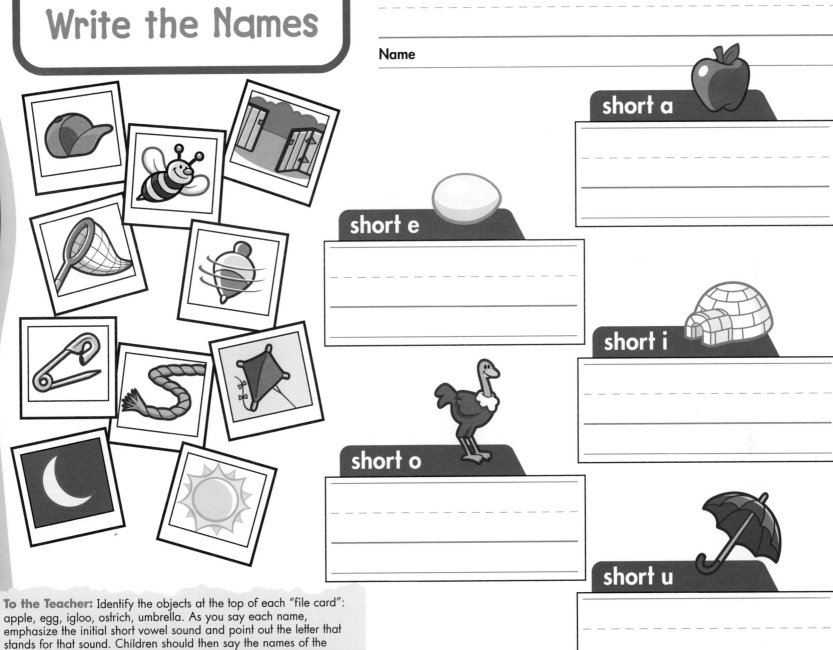

Writing Readiness:
Short Vowel Sounds

Write the Names

Name _____

short a

short e

short i

short o

short u

Choose the Pictures

2+3=5

To the Teacher: This activity prepares the child to gather information. Explain that Brad wants to tell a friend in another state about his school. He plans to send his friend some pictures and a letter telling about the pictures. Brad's first job is to decide which pictures to send. On this page are some pictures Brad took. The envelope has room for only four pictures. Ask children to write the letter **s** next to Brad's pictures from school and the letter **h** next to Brad's pictures from home. Have them share their responses and give the reasons for their choices. Remind children that Brad will send only four "school" pictures. See the Teacher Edition for more activities.

Write About It

Name

My School

To the Teacher: This activity prepares the child to organize information to make a web. Before beginning this activity, be sure all children agree on the four pictures from page 24. Tell children they will use the web on this page to sort the pictures and say something about each one. Call attention to the words *My School* in the center of the web. Remind them that this is the topic. Have children choose one of the "s" or "school" pictures on the facing page and write a word or two about it in one of the yellow boxes. (Accept developmental spelling.) Children should then repeat the process with the other three pictures they have chosen. See the Teacher Edition for more activities.

Complete the Letter

Dear Ted,

_____

- - - - - - - - - - - - - -

My job is _____

_____

- - - - - - - - - - - - - -

_____.

_____

I feed her every few days. Her bowl must be

_____

- - - - - - - - - - - - - -

kept clean. I _____

_____

- - - - - - - - - - - - - -

_____.

_____

Your pal,
Brad

Writing Readiness:
Making Sentences
Pick and Write

Name _____

Telling Sentence

Kip

.

Asking Sentence

Can

?

To the Teacher: Call attention to the orange tree and to the word in each orange. Ask volunteers to say the words one at a time. Provide assistance as needed. Explain that these words can be used to make a sentence that makes a statement, but they have to be put in the right order. Have children use the words to write a telling sentence. Call attention to the capital letter on the first word and the period at the end of the sentence. Explain that by changing the places of two words, the sentence can be made into a question. Complete the activity. Note the capital letter on the first word and the question mark at the end of the asking sentence. See the Teacher Edition for more activities.

Join the Parts

Doer (Subject)	Action (Verb)
The fat hen	puts nuts in the bag.
My kite	ate the corn.
Ken	go fast.
The red fox	is in the tree.
Jets	hid in a hole.

To the Teacher: Tell children that this is an activity sheet Tish got when she went to a restaurant. They will complete the activity by matching a puzzle piece in the first column with a puzzle piece in the second column to make a sentence. Have children draw lines to connect them. Demonstrate with the first piece: *The fat hen ate the corn.* Read the sentence once the piece is put together. Point out the doer (subject) and the action (verb). After completing all of the sentences, have children write one on the write-on lines. See the Teacher Edition for more activities.

Write the Words

Name

My Trip to the Store

Mom and I went to the store last week. _____ drove to the

store in our van. I _____ a bag and put purple grapes in it.

Then I _____ it in our cart. _____ wanted to eat

grapes that day. Going to the store was fun.

To the Teacher: Tell children they will read a story, but it is missing some words: subjects and verbs. Explain that these types of words are necessary. Tell children that they need to supply the missing words. Call on a volunteer to read the title. Allow children to predict what the paragraph is about. Then have another volunteer read the paragraph, saying the word "blank" when he/she reaches the space and stopping at the end of the sentence. Children can then be told to write the missing word, or if you prefer, the class can discuss possible words before writing. Accept any word that fits the meaning and is grammatically compatible with the sentence. See the Teacher Edition for more activities.

Writing Process Readiness:
Prewriting → Gather

Make a List

Choose Foods

Name

fruit

vegetable

meat

I like _____ because

_____ .

To the Teacher: This activity prepares the child to organize information to make a spider map. Help children name the foods that Tish likes. Point out that they are fruits, vegetables, and meats. Explain that the children must now choose the food they like the best in each food group. The spider map will help them. Begin by having children write the word *food* in the center box. Guide them to see that the three legs of the spider map name three food groups. Have children sound out and write the names of the foods they like the best on the correct lines. (Accept developmental spelling.) Then have children talk about their choices and reasons and complete the sentence at the bottom of the page. See the Teacher Edition for more activities.

31

Match the Pictures

because

.

To the Teacher: This activity prepares the child to revise information to make cause and effect statements. Children will match the pictures by drawing lines. Before starting, ask children about each picture. Point out that in the first picture in the left column, Tish is drinking a glass of orange juice. Then help children make a "cause and effect" relationship by finding the picture that matches in the right column. "Tish is drinking orange juice because Mom squeezed the oranges." Ask children to match and discuss the other pictures. Guide them in writing a "cause and effect" sentence about **one** pair of pictures on the write-on lines. Emphasize the word *because,* which children will use in Unit 6 when they do persuasive writing. See the Teacher Edition for more activities.

NARRATIVE

Writing to Tell a Story

1

A Story About Me

2

A Letter to My Best Friend

Theme: My Family and Friends

A Story About Me

PERSONAL NARRATIVE

Hi, I'm Yan. Do you like stories? I do. I love hearing stories. I like telling them and writing them, too! I want to show you a story I wrote. It's a story about me.

I always use this list to write good stories about me.

Personal Story Writing Checklist

☑ Tell a story about me.

☑ Tell what happened first, next, and last.

☑ Take out words that don't belong.

☑ Start each sentence with a capital letter.

☑ Make the word **I** a capital letter.

Here's the story I wrote about me.

My Day at the Park
by Yan

One day my family went to the park. I helped put food and drinks on the picnic table. Then it began to rain very hard! We had to eat in our car. We didn't have much room, but it was dry. It was fun eating in the car.

To the Teacher: Invite volunteers to read all or part of the story. Discuss the events in Yan's story with the group. Then discuss the checklist questions on page 37.

Directions: Talk about the questions. Circle **yes** or **no** to show if Yan followed the Personal Story Writing Checklist.

Personal Story Writing Checklist Questions

✓	Does the story tell about me?	yes	no
✓	Does the story tell what happened first, next, and last?	yes	no
✓	Does the story have words that don't belong?	yes	no
✓	Does each sentence start with a capital letter?	yes	no
✓	Is the word **I** a capital letter?	yes	no

Gather Ideas

Think of ideas for my story. Pick one.

Did you like my story? I can tell you how I wrote it. The first thing I did was think of things I could write about. I thought about some fun days. Look on the next page. Each picture I drew reminds me of a fun day.

To the Teacher: Read the text aloud to the children. Look at the pictures on page 39. Have children speculate and discuss what the stories Yan recalled are about and why Yan chose to write about the picnic at the park.

- Picture of cookies reminds Yan of making cookies.
- Picture of park entrance reminds Yan of a picnic.

Gather Ideas

Think of ideas for my story. Pick one.

I chose to write about my picnic at the park. That was a fun day! Now it's your turn. Think of some fun days you have had. What would you like to write about?

To the Teacher: Read the text aloud to the children. Help children recall two fun days in their lives. Then have them draw a picture that reminds them of each day. Tell children that each picture will represent a story topic. One picture should go on page 41. The other picture should go on page 42.

Your Own Writing
Prewriting

Directions: Draw a picture of something that reminds you of a fun day you have had.

Your Own Writing
Prewriting

Name _____

Directions: Draw a picture of something that reminds you of another fun day you have had.

Directions: Now choose the picture you want to write a story about. Circle that picture.

To the Teacher: Have children circle their topic picture. Read page 43 with the children. Then reread Yan's story, "My Day at the Park," on page 36. Have children discuss whether Yan's storyboard pictures on page 43 tell the same story.

42

Make a Plan

**Plan my story.
Make a storyboard.**

First Part of Yan's Story **Next Part of Yan's Story** **Last Part of Yan's Story**

To plan my story, I drew pictures. They made a storyboard. It shows what happened first, next, and last at the picnic.

Your Own Writing
Prewriting

Directions: Draw a picture to show what happened in the first part of your story.

First Part of My Story
(First Picture on My Storyboard)

To the Teacher: Ask children to tear out pages 41 and 42. Work with the children to tell orally the story about their chosen topic picture. Then, based on their topic picture, have children draw a picture on this page that "tells" about the first part of their fun day. On page 45, have children "tell" about the next part of their fun day by drawing a second picture.

Your Own Writing
Prewriting

Name

Directions: Draw a picture to show what happened in the next part of your story.

Next Part of My Story
(Next Picture on My Storyboard)

Your Own Writing
Prewriting

Directions: Draw a picture to show what happened in the last part of your story.

Last Part of My Story
(Last Picture on My Storyboard)

To the Teacher: Have children "tell" about the last part of their fun day by drawing a third picture on this page. Read page 47 with the children.

46

Write

**Use my storyboard.
Write my story.**

Next, I used my plan to write a draft of my story. A draft is for getting your ideas down. On the next pages, you'll see how I wrote mine. Then you can write your draft, too!

Drafting

Write

Use my storyboard. Write the first part of my story.

First Picture on Yan's Storyboard

This is what I wrote about my first picture.

First Part of Yan's Story

one day my family went to the park. i helped put stuff like food and drinks on the picnic table.

Name

Directions: Tear out page 44. Look at the picture you drew in the green box. Write about the picture to draft the first part of your story.

DRAFT

First Part of My Story

Write

Use my storyboard. Write the next part of my story.

Next Picture on Yan's Storyboard

Next Part of Yan's Story

This is what I wrote about my next picture.

then it began to rain very hard! It rained last week, too.

To the Teacher: Read page 50. As children write their drafts, make sure the text in each section relates to the corresponding picture on their storyboard. Tell children to tear out page 45 to draft on page 51. After children use torn-out page 45, remind them to keep it in a safe place. They will need the back, page 46, to finish their drafts.

50

Your Own Writing
Drafting

Name

Directions: Tear out page 45. Look at the picture you drew in the yellow box. Write about the picture to draft the next part of your story.

Next Part of My Story

DRAFT

Drafting
Write
Use my storyboard. Write the last part of my story.

Last Picture on Yan's Storyboard

Last Part of Yan's Story

DRAFT

This is what I wrote about my last picture.

We had to eat in our car. We didn't have much room, but it was dry. It was fun eating in the car.

To the Teacher: Read page 52. As children prepare to write the last part of their stories on page 53, remind them that page 46 is on the back of page 45.

52

Your Own Writing
Drafting

Directions: Look at the picture you drew in the red box on page 46. Write about the picture to draft the last part of your story.

Last Part of My Story

DRAFT

My Day at the Park

one day my family went to the park. i helped put stuff like food and drinks on the picnic table. then it began to rain very hard! It rained last week, too. We had to eat in our car. We didn't have much room, but it was dry. It was fun eating in the car.

Here's my whole story!

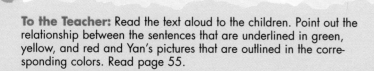

To the Teacher: Read the text aloud to the children. Point out the relationship between the sentences that are underlined in green, yellow, and red and Yan's pictures that are outlined in the corresponding colors. Read page 55.

54

Read My Paper

Take out words that don't belong.

Next, I read my paper. I thought about what I wrote. Then I thought about the changes I could make. I wanted to make my story even better. The next two pages show what I did.

Read My Paper

Take out words that don't belong.

I took out words that didn't fit.
I crossed them out. Here's why I
made changes.

1. I crossed out "stuff like."
   That isn't needed.
2. I crossed out "It rained last week, too."
   That doesn't tell about the day.

To the Teacher: Read why Yan made changes. Then read Yan's revised story on page 57. Ask children to point to what Yan crossed out. Discuss whether Yan's changes improved her story and why.

My Day at the Park

one day my family went to the park. i helped put ~~stuff like~~ food and drinks on the picnic table. then it began to rain very hard! ~~It rained last week, too.~~ We had to eat in our car. We didn't have much room, but it was dry. It was fun eating in the car.

Your Own Writing
Revising

My Revising Steps

Step 1 Read my story out loud or to myself.

Step 2 Look for places where I need to take out words. Are there any words that don't fit? Cross out those words.

Step 3 Read my story again. Is it better?

To the Teacher: Read the directions with the children. Have them revise the drafts of the story they wrote on pages 49, 51, and 53. Remind children to tear out pages 49–53. Tell them that they may read their stories out loud or to themselves. After revising, read page 59 with the children.

Next, I needed to edit my story with the help of a partner. But before I did that, I learned this good tip on how to talk with my partner.

Talk With a Partner Tip

Let your partner see your paper as you read it.

Read your paper out loud to your partner.

Ask your partner for suggestions.

Editing

Proofread

Fix mistakes in capital letters.

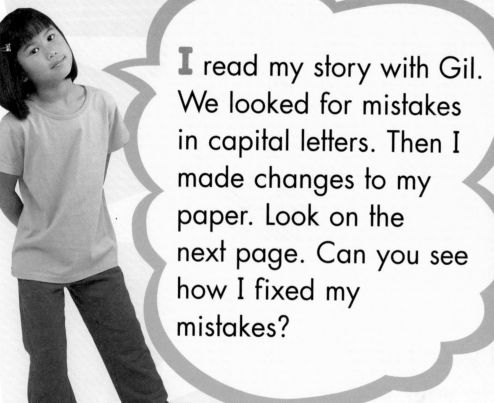

I read my story with Gil. We looked for mistakes in capital letters. Then I made changes to my paper. Look on the next page. Can you see how I fixed my mistakes?

Skills

Capital Letters

- Always start a new sentence with a **capital letter**.

- Always write the word **I** as a **capital letter**.

Proofreading Mark

Draw three lines under a letter to show that it should be a capital letter.

DRAFT

My Day at the Park

~~O~~ one day my family went
to the park. ~~i~~ I helped put
~~stuff like~~ food and drinks
on the picnic table. ~~t~~ T then it
began to rain very hard! ~~It
rained last week, too.~~ We
had to eat in our car. We
didn't have much room, but
it was dry. It was fun
eating in the car.

Your Own Writing
Editing

Directions: Read the draft
you wrote on pages 49–53.
Fix mistakes. Use the
checklist questions on
page 37, too.

Publishing

Share

Post my story in my classroom.

Now I was ready to share my story. I copied it onto a clean sheet of paper. I put my name on it. I made all the changes and used my best handwriting. Then I pasted my story onto heavy red paper. That made it look special!

Your Own Writing
Publishing

Directions: Copy your story onto a clean sheet of paper.

My Day at the Park
by Yan

One day my family went to the park. I helped put food and drinks on the picnic table. Then it began to rain very hard! We had to eat in our car. We didn't have much room, but it was dry. It was fun eating in the car.

A Letter to My Best Friend

Hi, my name is Alicia. My best friend lives far away. We write letters to each other. I'm going to show you a letter I wrote. It tells about a place I visited.

To the Teacher: Read the text aloud to the children. Introduce Alicia. Discuss why people write letters. Explain that Alicia has written a letter to tell her friend about a place Alicia visited. Read page 65.

I always use this list to write good letters.

Letter Writing Checklist

☑ Use these three parts: greeting, body, closing.

☑ Tell my reader something interesting.

☑ Tell what happened first, next, and last.

☑ Take out words that don't belong.

☑ Start each sentence with a capital letter.

☑ Make the word **I** a capital letter.

☑ Start the name of a person or place with a capital letter.

This is the letter about the place I visited.

Dear Beth,

I went to the Hampton Zoo. My dad took me last week. We saw an elephant named Sadie. She was five years old. She ate peanuts from the trainer's hand! I had fun at the zoo.

Your friend,

Alicia

MODEL
FRIENDLY LETTER

Directions: Talk about the questions. Circle **yes** or **no** to show if Alicia followed the Letter Writing Checklist.

Letter Writing Checklist Questions

☑	Does the letter have a greeting, a body, and a closing?	yes	no
☑	Did I tell something interesting?	yes	no
☑	Does the letter tell what happened first, next, and last?	yes	no
☑	Does the letter have words that don't belong?	yes	no
☑	Does each sentence start with a capital letter?	yes	no
☑	Is the word **I** a capital letter?	yes	no
☑	Does the name of a person or place start with a capital letter?	yes	no

Prewriting
Gather Ideas

Think of ideas for my letter. Pick one.

What did you think of my letter? Here's how I wrote it. First, I thought of things I could write about. I thought about great places I have visited. Then I drew two pictures. Each picture reminds me of a place. Look on the next page.

Prewriting
Gather Ideas

Think of ideas for my letter. Pick one.

I knew Beth had never been to the zoo. So I decided to write and tell her about it. Now it's your turn. Think of some great places you have visited. Which place would you like to write about? Who would you like to tell?

To the Teacher: Read the text aloud. Help children recall two different places they have visited and enjoyed. Then have them draw a picture that reminds them of each place. Tell children that each picture will represent a story topic. One picture should go on page 71. The other picture should go on page 72.

Your Own Writing
Prewriting

Name

Directions: Draw a picture of something that reminds you of a great place you have visited.

Your Own Writing
Prewriting

Name

Directions: Draw a picture of something that reminds you of another great place you have visited.

Directions: Now choose the picture you want to write about in a letter. Circle that picture.

Prewriting

Make a Plan
Plan my letter.
Make a storyboard.

First Part of Alicia's Letter

Next Part of Alicia's Letter

Last Part of Alicia's Letter

To plan my letter, I made a storyboard. The pictures I drew show what happened first, next, and last at the zoo.

Your Own Writing
Prewriting

Name _____

Directions: Draw a picture to show what happened first.

First Part of My Letter
(First Picture on My Storyboard)

To the Teacher: Ask children to tear out pages 71 and 72. Work with the children to tell orally what happened in their chosen topic picture. Then, based on their topic picture, have children draw a picture on this page that "tells" about the first part of their visit to this great place. On page 75, have children "tell" about the next part of their visit by drawing a second picture.

74

Your Own Writing
Prewriting

Directions: Draw a picture to show what happened next.

Next Part of My Letter
(Next Picture on My Storyboard)

Your Own Writing
Prewriting

Name

Directions: Draw a picture to show what happened last.

Last Part of My Letter
(Last Picture on My Storyboard)

To the Teacher: Have children "tell" about the last part of their visit by drawing a third picture on this page. Read page 77 with the children.

76

Drafting
Write

**Use my storyboard.
Write my letter.**

Next, I used my plan to write a draft of my letter. I wrote my friend's name first. Then I wrote my ideas down. I even signed my name at the end of my letter. Look on the next pages to see what I did. You can do this, too!

Drafting
Write

Use my storyboard. Write the first part of my letter.

First Picture on Alicia's Storyboard

I wrote my greeting. Then I wrote about my first picture.

Alicia's Greeting

Dear beth,

First Part of Alicia's Letter

I went to the hampton zoo. My dad took me last week.

To the Teacher: Read page 78. Help children see the relationship between Alicia's picture (or plan) and her draft. Errors in proper nouns are intentional; children will learn to capitalize them later. Tell children to tear out page 74 so they can refer to their storyboard picture while they draft on page 79. Remind children to write a greeting at the beginning of their letter.

Name

Directions: Tear out page 74. Look at the picture you drew in the green box. Write about the picture.

DRAFT

Dear   ,

My Greeting

First Part of My Letter

Drafting
Write
Use my storyboard. Write the next part of my letter.

Next Picture on Alicia's Storyboard

Next Part of Alicia's Letter

Here's what I wrote about my next picture.

We saw an elephant named Sadie. She was five years old. My brother is five years old.

To the Teacher: Read page 80. As children write their drafts, make sure the text in each section relates to the corresponding picture on their storyboard. Tell children to tear out page 75 to draft on page 81. After children use torn-out page 75, remind them to keep it in a safe place. They will need the back, page 76, to finish their drafts.

Your Own Writing
Drafting

Name

Directions: Tear out page 75. Look at the picture you drew in the yellow box. Write about the picture.

Next Part of My Letter

Drafting
Write
Use my storyboard. Write the last part of my letter.

Last Picture on Alicia's Storyboard

Last Part of Alicia's Letter

She ate peanuts right out from the trainer's hand! I had fun at the zoo.

I wrote about my last picture. Then I wrote my closing with my name.

Alicia's Closing

Your friend, Alicia

To the Teacher: Read page 82. As children prepare to write the last part of their letters on page 83, remind them that page 76 is on the back of page 75. Make sure children write a closing at the end of their letters.

82

Your Own Writing
Drafting

Name

Directions: Look at the picture you drew in the red box on page 76. Write about the picture.

Last Part of My Letter

My Closing

,

Dear beth,
    I went to the hampton zoo. My dad took me last week. We saw an elephant named Sadie. She was five years old. My brother is five years old. She ate peanuts right out from the trainer's hand! I had fun at the zoo.

        Your friend,
Alicia

Do you like my letter?

To the Teacher: Read the text aloud. Point out the relationship between the sentences that are underlined in green, yellow, and red and Alicia's pictures that are outlined in the corresponding colors. Point out the greeting and the closing that are underlined in blue. Read page 85.

84

Read My Paper

Take out words that don't belong.

Next, I read my paper. This helped me think about what I wrote and how I could make my letter even better. The next two pages show the changes I made.

Read My Paper

Take out words that don't belong.

I crossed out words that didn't fit. This is why I made changes.

1. I crossed out "My brother is five years old." That doesn't tell anything about the zoo!

2. I crossed out "right out." That isn't needed.

To the Teacher: Read why Alicia made changes. Then read Alicia's revised letter on page 87. Ask children to point to what Alicia crossed out. Discuss whether Alicia's changes improved her letter and why.

Dear beth,

 I went to the hampton zoo. My dad took me last week. We saw an elephant named Sadie. She was five years old. ~~My brother is five years old.~~ She ate peanuts ~~right out~~ from the trainer's hand! I had fun at the zoo.

Your friend,
Alicia

Your Own Writing
Revising

Directions: Tear out pages 79–83. Read the letter you wrote. Use the steps below to check your draft.

My Revising Steps

Step 1 — Read my letter out loud or to myself.

Step 2 — Look for places where I need to take out words. Are there any words that don't fit? Cross out those words.

Step 3 — Read my letter again. Is it better?

To the Teacher: Read the directions with the children. Have them revise the drafts of the letter they wrote on pages 79, 81, and 83. Remind children to tear out pages 79–83. Tell them that they may read their letters out loud or to themselves. After revising, read page 89 with the children.

ORAL LANGUAGE
Talk
With a Partner
COOPERATIVE LEARNING

Next, I was ready to edit my letter with the help of a partner. But before I started, I learned this tip about working with my partner.

Talk With a Partner Tip

After reading your paper out loud, ask your partner how you can make it better.

Listen to your partner, but write on your own paper.

You should write the changes you want to make. Your partner shouldn't write the changes for you.

Proofread

Fix mistakes in capital letters.

As I read my letter with Joe, we checked for capital letter mistakes. I used the proofreading mark to show changes. Look on the next page to see how I fixed my mistakes.

Capital Letters

- Always start a new sentence with a **capital letter**.
- Always write the word **I** as a **capital letter**.
- Always start the name of a person or place with a **capital letter**.

Proofreading Mark

Draw three lines under a letter to show that it should be a capital letter.

DRAFT

Dear B̲beth,
   I went to the H̲hampton
Z̲zoo. My dad took me last
week. We saw an elephant
named Sadie. She was five
years old. ~~My brother is~~
~~five years old.~~ She ate
peanuts ~~right out~~ from the
trainer's hand! I had fun at
the zoo.

            Your friend,
            Alicia

Your Own Writing
Editing

Directions: Read the draft you wrote on pages 79–83. Fix mistakes. Use the checklist questions on page 67, too.

Publishing

Share   **Mail my letter to my friend.**

My last step was to make a neat copy of my letter. I made all the changes. I used my best handwriting, and I drew a picture! I even signed my name. Then I addressed an envelope to my friend. I sent her my letter.

Your Own Writing
Publishing

Directions: Copy your letter onto a clean sheet of paper.

Dear Beth,

   I went to the Hampton Zoo. My dad took me last week. We saw an elephant named Sadie. She was five years old. She ate peanuts from the trainer's hand! I had fun at the zoo.

Your friend,
Alicia

Your Own Writing
NARRATIVE

Directions: Use the strategies from this unit. Write a personal story or a friendly letter. Pick an idea below. Use this idea for your own paper. Follow the steps in the writing process. Use the checklists to check your writing.

PERSONAL NARRATIVE

Write about a time you went to a birthday party.

FRIENDLY LETTER

Write to a relative about a time you got a new pet.

School–Home Connection

portfolio

Keep a writing folder. Take your writing folder home to share.

DESCRIPTIVE

Writing to Describe

1 Description of Two People

2 Description of Two Places

Theme: My Neighborhood

Description of Two People

Hi, I'm Rick. I have two neighbors named Patty and Glen. I wrote a descriptive paper to tell about them. A descriptive paper is like a picture. Only instead of using crayons to make the picture, you use words!

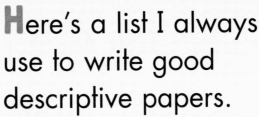

Here's a list I always use to write good descriptive papers.

Descriptive Writing Checklist

☑ Tell what someone or something is like.

☑ Use words that tell what people look like.

☑ Change or add words to make my paper better.

☑ Start each sentence with a capital letter.

☑ Use a period at the end of a telling sentence.

This is my paper. It tells about Patty and Glen.

My Neighbors
by Rick

Patty and Glen are my neighbors. They are both very friendly. They always smile at me. Patty is a young lady. She is tall. Her brown hair is long. Glen is an older man. He is short. His gray hair is curly.

MODEL
DESCRIPTIVE PAPER

To the Teacher: Invite volunteers to read all or part of Rick's paper. With the group, discuss the descriptive words Rick used, i.e., *friendly, young, tall, older, short*. Then discuss the checklist questions on page 99.

Descriptive Writing Checklist Questions

☑	Does the paper tell what someone or something is like?	yes	no
☑	Does the paper have words that tell what people look like?	yes	no
☑	Does the paper need to have any words changed or added?	yes	no
☑	Does each sentence start with a capital letter?	yes	no
☑	Is there a period at the end of each telling sentence?	yes	no

Gather Ideas

**Draw two people I know.
List words to tell about them.**

I'll tell you how I wrote my paper. The first thing I did was think of people I could write about.

Then I drew a picture of each person. I made a list of words to tell about each person. I wasn't sure how to spell **neighbor,** so I asked my teacher. Look at the next page to see my pictures and word lists.

To the Teacher: Read the text aloud to the children. Look at the pictures on page 101. Ask children to speculate why Rick decided to write about these two people. Discuss with the group how the words in each list describe the person in the picture.

lady
neighbor
young
tall
brown hair
friendly

man
older
short
gray hair
neighbor
friendly

I chose to write about two neighbors. Now it's your turn to write.

Name

Directions: Draw a picture of a person you know. List words to tell about that person.

To the Teacher: Help children think of two people they know. Then have them draw a picture of each person. One picture should go on page 102. The other picture should go on page 103. Ask children to list words to tell about each person.

Your Own Writing
Prewriting

Directions: Draw a picture of another person you know. List words to tell about that person.

Prewriting
Make a Plan

Plan my paper. Use my pictures and word lists to make a Venn diagram.

To plan my paper, I made a Venn diagram. I drew one pink circle and one blue circle. The circles overlapped, so the middle lines turned purple!

You can see my Venn on page 106. It shows how my two neighbors are the same and how they are different.

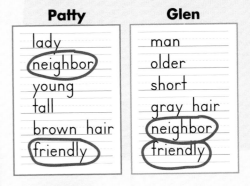

Patty

lady
(neighbor)
young
tall
brown hair
(friendly)

Glen

man
older
short
gray hair
(neighbor)
(friendly)

After I drew my Venn diagram, I looked at my word lists on page 101. I circled the words that are the same. I wrote them in the purple part of my Venn.

Then I wrote the other words from the pink box in the pink part of the Venn. I wrote the other words from the blue box in the blue part of the Venn. Turn the page to see my Venn.

Make a Plan

Plan my paper. Use my pictures and word lists to make a Venn diagram.

Rick's Venn Diagram

Patty
lady
young
tall
brown hair

Both
neighbor
friendly

Glen
man
older
short
gray hair

To the Teacher: Discuss the Venn diagram with the children. Have them look back at the lists and pictures on page 101. Point out that the outer sections list characteristics that are unique to each person (differences) and the middle section lists characteristics they share (similarities). Read page 107 with the children.

My Venn diagram helped me list ways that my neighbors are the same and ways that they are different.

Now it's your turn. Make a Venn diagram. Show how the people you chose are the same and different.

Your Own Writing
Prewriting

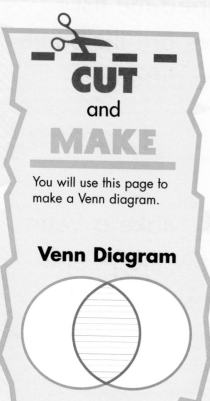

✂️
CUT
and
MAKE

You will use this page to
make a Venn diagram.

Venn Diagram

Name _____

Directions: Tear out pages 102 and 103. Circle the
words that are the same on both lists. Write the circled
words below to tell how your two people are the same.

Both

(Middle)

Cut here.

To the Teacher: Ask children to tear out pages 102 and 103. Work with
the children to tell orally about the two people they have chosen. Then
have them complete the purple section of the Venn diagram on this page
and the pink section on page 109. Ask children to label the pink section
with the name of the first person they are writing about. Tell children they
will cut out and assemble their Venn diagram later. When cutting,
make sure children start at "Cut here." and stay on the dotted lines.

Name

Directions: Look at your pink box. Write words that tell about your first person only.

CUT and MAKE

You will use this page to make a Venn diagram.

Venn Diagram

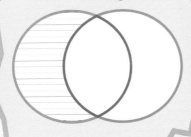

(Left Side of Venn)

Cut here.

Your Own Writing
Prewriting

✂

⬛ ▬ CUT ▬ ⬛
and
MAKE

You will use this page to make a Venn diagram.

Venn Diagram

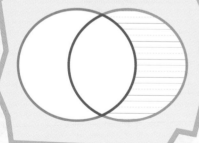

Name _____

Directions: Look at your blue box. Write words that tell about your second person only.

(Right Side of Venn)

Cut here. ✂

110

Drafting
Write

Use my Venn diagram.
Write how the people are the same.
Write how the people are different.

Next, I wrote my draft. I looked at my Venn diagram a lot. This gave me good ideas! Remember, a draft is a chance to put your ideas on paper. You can fix mistakes later.

Drafting Write

Use my Venn diagram.
Write how the people are the same.
Write how the people are different.

Read my draft on the next page.

Rick's Venn Diagram

Patty
lady
young
tall
brown hair

Both
neighbor
friendly

Glen
man
older
short
gray hair

To the Teacher: Read page 112. Explain the relationship between Rick's Venn diagram (or plan) and his draft. On page 113, point out the connection between the sentences that are underlined in purple, pink, and blue and the sections of Rick's Venn diagram that are outlined in the corresponding colors.

My Neighbors

Patty and Glen are the neighbors. They are both very friendly They always smile at me. Patty is a lady. She is tall. Her hair is long. Glen is an older man. He is short His gray hair is curly.

Now it's your turn.

Your Own Writing
Drafting

Name

Directions: Use the words in the purple part of your Venn diagram to write sentences about how both people are the same.

DRAFT

How My Two People Are the Same

To the Teacher: On this page, have children write about how their people are the same. On page 115, have them write about how their first person is different from their second person. Children should have their Venn diagram beside them. Point out the color relationship between the parts of the Venn and the outlines of the drafting boxes.

114

Your Own Writing
Drafting

DRAFT

Name

Directions: Use the words in the pink part of your Venn diagram to write sentences about your first person only.

How My First Person Is Different

Your Own Writing
Drafting

Name

Directions: Use the words in the blue part of your Venn diagram to write sentences about your second person only.

How My Second Person Is Different

DRAFT

To the Teacher: On this page, have children write about how their second person is different from their first person. Children should have their Venn diagram beside them. Read page 117 with the children.

116

Read My Paper

Change or add words to make my paper better.

How did I make my paper even better? First, I read it. Then I thought about how I could revise it. The next two pages show what I did.

Revising

Read My Paper

Change or add words to make my paper better.

I changed one word and added some other words. Here's why I made changes.

1. I changed "the" to "my." It tells that the neighbors are mine.
2. I added "young" and "brown." These words describe Patty and her hair.

DRAFT

My Neighbors

Patty and Glen are ~~the~~ my neighbors. They are both very friendly They always smile at me. Patty is a young lady. She is tall. Her brown hair is long. Glen is an older man. He is short His gray hair is curly.

Your Own Writing
Revising

My Revising Steps

Step 1 Read my paper out loud or to myself.

Step 2 Look for places where I can tell more about a person. Change or add words to tell more.

Step 3 Read my paper again. Is it better?

To the Teacher: Read the directions with the children. Have them tear out pages 114–116 and revise the drafts of the paper they wrote. After revising, read page 121 with the children.

ORAL LANGUAGE

Talk With a partner

COOPERATIVE LEARNING

Before I edited my paper with my partner, I learned this tip. It's important so we won't disturb others!

Talk With a Partner Tip

Speak in soft voices.

Use soft voices and sit close together. You will hear your partner but will not disturb others.

Editing

Proofread

Use a period at the end of a telling sentence.

I read my paper with Kenji. We looked for periods. Then I put in the missing ones. On the next page, you can see how I fixed my mistakes.

Periods

Always use a **period** at the end of a telling sentence.

Proofreading Mark

⊙

Draw a period inside a circle. This shows where the period should be added.

To the Teacher: Read the text aloud to the children. Explain the skill and the proofreading mark. Ask children to look at page 123 and find the changes Rick made to his paper. Then have children read their drafts and fix their mistakes.

My Neighbors

Patty and Glen are the ~~the~~ *my* neighbors. They are both very friendly. They always smile at me. Patty is a *young* lady. She is tall. Her *brown* hair is long. Glen is an older man. He is short. His gray hair is curly.

Your Own Writing
Editing

Directions: Read the draft you wrote on pages 114–116. Fix mistakes. Use the checklist questions on page 99, too.

Publishing

Share

Make a class book.

Now I was ready to make a clean copy of my paper. I made all the changes and used my best handwriting. I wrote my name, too. My paper was ready for my classmates to read. I couldn't wait to see everyone's papers in a class book!

Your Own Writing
Publishing

Directions: Copy your descriptive paper onto a clean sheet of paper.

To the Teacher: Read the text on pages 124 and 125 aloud. Have children publish their descriptive papers on separate paper. Then help them use the checklist questions on page 99 to assess their writing. Bind children's work together in a class book.

124

My Neighbors
by Rick

Patty and Glen are my neighbors. They are both very friendly. They always smile at me. Patty is a young lady. She is tall. Her brown hair is long. Glen is an older man. He is short. His gray hair is curly.

Description of Two Places

Hi, my name is Allen. I wrote a descriptive paper to tell about two places near my house—the playground and the swimming pool. I want to show you the paper I wrote.

To the Teacher: Read the text aloud to the children. Introduce Allen. Discuss why people write descriptive papers. Explain that Allen has written a paper telling how the playground and the swimming pool are the same and how they are different. Read page 127.

This list always helps me write good descriptive papers.

Descriptive Writing Checklist

☑ Tell what someone or something is like.

☑ Use words that tell what places look like.

☑ Change or add words to make my paper better.

☑ Start each sentence with a capital letter.

☑ Use a period at the end of a telling sentence.

☑ Use a question mark at the end of an asking sentence.

Here's my paper. It tells about two places in my neighborhood.

My Favorite Places
by Allen

The playground and the swimming pool are two places to have fun. They both have slides. The playground has swings. It has green grass and trees. The pool has a diving board and steps. It has cool water. Do you like the playground or the swimming pool the best?

MODEL
DESCRIPTIVE PAPER

Descriptive Writing Checklist Questions

☑	Does the paper tell what someone or something is like?	yes	no
☑	Does the paper have words that tell what places look like?	yes	no
☑	Does the paper need to have any words changed or added?	yes	no
☑	Does each sentence start with a capital letter?	yes	no
☑	Is there a period at the end of each telling sentence?	yes	no
☑	Is there a question mark at the end of each asking sentence?	yes	no

Prewriting
Gather Ideas

**Draw two places I know.
List words to tell about them.**

Here's how I wrote my paper. First, I thought of places I could write about. I thought about what each place was like. Then I drew a picture of each place.

I also wrote words to tell about each place. Look at my pictures and words on the next page.

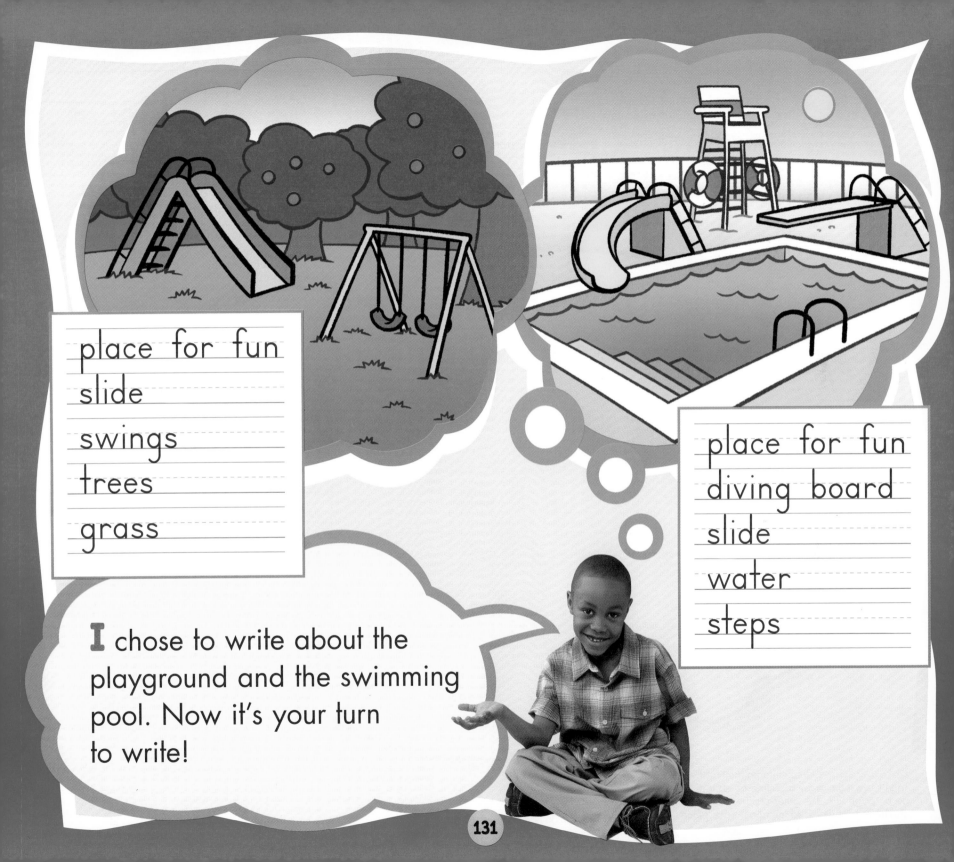

place for fun
slide
swings
trees
grass

place for fun
diving board
slide
water
steps

I chose to write about the playground and the swimming pool. Now it's your turn to write!

Your Own Writing
Prewriting

Name _____

Directions: Draw a picture of a place you know. List words to tell about that place.

Your Own Writing
Prewriting

Name

Directions: Draw a picture of another place you know. List words to tell about that place.

Prewriting
Make a Plan
Plan my paper. Use my pictures and word lists to make a Venn diagram.

Next, I drew a Venn diagram to plan my paper. Do you remember how to make a Venn? Well, I drew two circles—a pink one and a blue one. The part that overlapped made purple.

Look at my Venn diagram on page 136. You'll see how my two places are the same and how they are different.

To the Teacher: Read the text aloud to the children. Remind them what a Venn diagram looks like and why it is used. Have children look at Allen's Venn on page 136. Read page 135 together.

I drew my Venn diagram. Then I used my word lists from page 131. I circled the words that are the same. I wrote those words in the purple part of my Venn.

I wrote the other words from the pink box in the pink part of the Venn. I wrote the other words from the blue box in the blue part of the Venn. See my Venn on the next page.

Playground

place for fun
slide
swings
trees
grass

Swimming Pool

place for fun
diving board
slide
water
steps

Make a Plan

Plan my paper. Use my pictures and word lists to make a Venn diagram.

Allen's Venn Diagram

Playground

swings

trees

grass

Both

place for fun

slide

Swimming Pool

diving board

water

steps

To the Teacher: Discuss the Venn diagram with the children. Have them look back at the lists and pictures on page 131. Point out that the outer sections list characteristics that are unique to each place (differences) and the middle section lists characteristics they share (similarities). Read page 137 with the children.

On my Venn diagram, I was able to list ways that the playground and the swimming pool are the same and ways that they are different.

Can you make a Venn diagram to show how the places you chose are the same and different?

Your Own Writing
Prewriting

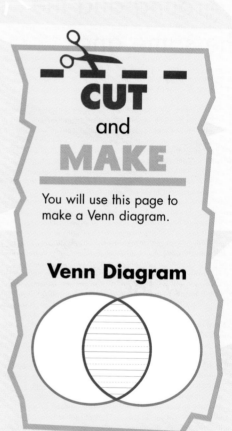
Name

Directions: Tear out pages 132 and 133. Circle the words that are the same on both lists. Write the circled words below to tell how your two places are the same.

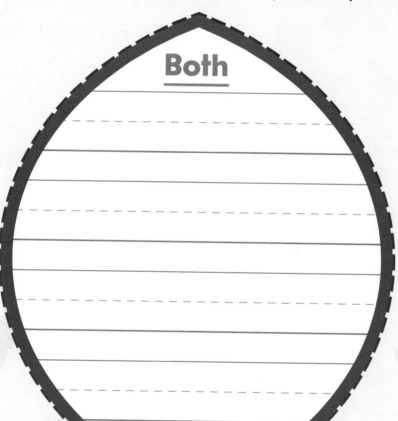

Both

(Middle)

Cut here.

To the Teacher: Ask children to tear out pages 132 and 133. Work with the children to tell orally about the two places they have chosen. Then have them complete the purple section of the Venn diagram on this page and the pink section on page 139. Ask children to label the pink section with the name of the first place they are writing about. Tell children they will cut out and assemble their Venn diagram later. When cutting, **make sure** children start at "Cut here." and stay on the dotted lines.

138

Your Own Writing
Prewriting

Directions: Look at your pink box. Write words that tell about your first place only.

CUT and MAKE

You will use this page to make a Venn diagram.

Venn Diagram

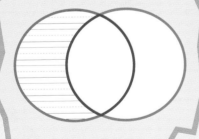

(Left Side of Venn)

Cut here.

139

Name

Directions: Look at your blue box. Write words that tell about your second place only.

CUT and MAKE

You will use this page to make a Venn diagram.

Venn Diagram

(Right Side of Venn)

To the Teacher: Have children complete and label the blue section of the Venn diagram on this page. Then help them tear out pages 138–140, cut out the Venn diagram, and paste it together onto a large, separate sheet of paper. When cutting, **make sure** children start at "Cut here." and stay on the dotted lines. Remember, pages 139 and 140 are back-to-back. Because the completed Venn diagram will be used for drafting, keep it in a safe place. Read page 141 with the children.

Cut here.

Drafting
Write

Use my Venn diagram.
Write how the places are the same.
Write how the places are different.

Next, I wrote my draft. I put the ideas from my Venn diagram into sentences. I didn't worry about making mistakes. I would have the chance to fix them later.

Drafting

Write

Use my Venn diagram.
Write how the places are the same.
Write how the places are different.

You can read my draft on the next page.

Allen's Venn Diagram

Playground
swings
trees
grass

Both
place for fun
slide

Swimming Pool
diving board
water
steps

To the Teacher: Read page 142. Explain the relationship between Allen's Venn diagram (or plan) and his draft. On page 143, point out the connection between the sentences that are underlined in purple, pink, and blue and the sections of Allen's Venn diagram that are outlined in the corresponding colors.

My Favorite Places

The playground and the swimming pool are two places to have fun. They both have slides. The playground has swings. It has grass and trees. The pool has a diving board and steps. It has water. Do you like the playground or the swimming pool the best

Are you ready to write?

Your Own Writing
Drafting

Name

Directions: Use the words in the purple part of your Venn diagram to write sentences about how both places are the same.

How My Two Places Are the Same

DRAFT

To the Teacher: On this page, have children write about how their places are the same. On page 145, have them write about how their first place is different from their second place. Children should have their Venn diagram beside them. Point out the color relationship between the parts of the Venn and the outlines of the drafting boxes.

Your Own Writing
Drafting

DRAFT

Directions: Use the words in the pink part of your Venn diagram to write sentences about your first place only.

How My First Place Is Different

Your Own Writing
Drafting

Name

Directions: Use the words in the blue part of your Venn diagram to write sentences about your second place only.

How My Second Place Is Different

DRAFT

To the Teacher: On this page, have children write about how their second place is different from their first place. Children should have their Venn diagram beside them. Read page 147 with the children.

146

Revising

Read My Paper

Change or add words to make my paper better.

Here's what I did next. I read my paper. I saw that I could make my paper even better if I changed some things! The next two pages show how I revised my paper.

Revising

Read My Paper

Change or add words to make my paper better.

I changed a word and added two more words. This is why I made changes.

1. I changed "two" to "both." It tells how the places are the same.
2. I added "green" and "cool." These words describe. They tell more about the places.

To the Teacher: Read why Allen made changes. Then read Allen's revised paper on page 149. Ask children to point to what Allen changed and added. Discuss whether Allen's changes improved his paper and why.

My Favorite Places

The playground and the swimming pool are ~~two~~ places to have fun. They both have slides. The playground has swings. It has grass and trees. The pool has a diving board and steps. It has water. Do you like the playground or the swimming pool the best

both

green

cool

Your Own Writing
Revising

Directions: Tear out the paper you wrote on pages 144–146. Use the steps below to check your draft.

My Revising Steps

Step 1 Read my paper out loud or to myself.

Step 2 Look for spots where I can tell more about a place. Change or add words to tell more.

Step 3 Read my paper again. Is it better?

To the Teacher: Read the directions with the children. Have them tear out pages 144–146 and revise the drafts of the paper they wrote. After revising, read page 151 with the children.

ORAL LANGUAGE
Talk
With a Partner
COOPERATIVE LEARNING

Here's a great tip I learned before I edited my paper with my partner. It's important so we can learn to share!

Talk With a Partner Tip

Take turns.

Don't do all the talking yourself. Everyone has something important to say. You and your partner should take turns talking and listening.

Editing

Proofread

Use a question mark at the end of an asking sentence.

After I read my paper with Sarah, we checked for question marks. I used the proofreading mark to show where to put a question mark. Look on the next page.

Skills

Question Marks

Always use a **question mark** at the end of an asking sentence.

Proofreading Mark

Draw a caret and a question mark to show where the question mark should be added.

A caret looks like this **∧**.

To the Teacher: Read the text aloud to the children. Explain the skill and the proofreading mark. Ask children to look at page 153 and find the change Allen made to his paper. Then have children read their drafts and fix their mistakes. Review period use at the end of a sentence.

My Favorite Places

The playground and the swimming pool are ~~two~~ places to have fun. They both have slides. The playground has swings. It has grass and trees. The pool has a diving board and steps. It has water. Do you like the playground or the swimming pool the best?

both

green

cool

Your Own Writing
Editing

Directions: Read the draft you wrote on pages 144–146. Fix mistakes. Use the checklist questions on page 129, too.

Publishing
Share

Read my paper aloud to a classmate.

The last thing I did was copy my paper neatly. I made all the changes and used my best handwriting. I even put my name on it. After I made all the changes, I knew my paper was ready for sharing! I read it out loud to a student in my class. She liked it!

Your Own Writing
Publishing

Directions: Copy your descriptive paper onto a clean sheet of paper.

To the Teacher: Read the text on pages 154 and 155 aloud. Have children publish their descriptive papers on separate paper or in a journal. Then help them use the checklist questions on page 129 to assess their writing. Invite each child to read his/her paper aloud to a classmate.

My Favorite Places
by Allen

The playground and the swimming pool are both places to have fun. They both have slides. The playground has swings. It has green grass and trees. The pool has a diving board and steps. It has cool water. Do you like the playground or the swimming pool the best?

Your Own Writing
DESCRIPTIVE

Directions: Use the strategies from this unit. Write a descriptive paper. Pick an idea below. Use this idea for your own paper. Follow the steps in the writing process. Use the checklists to check your writing.

DESCRIPTIVE PAPER

Write about two seasons you enjoy.

DESCRIPTIVE PAPER

Write about two kinds of animals you see in your neighborhood.

School–Home Connection

portfolio

Keep a writing folder. Take your writing folder home to share.

Writing to Give Information

1

Report on a Holiday

2

Report on a Hero

Theme: My Country

Report on a Holiday

FACTUAL REPORT

Hi, I'm Brad. Do you know what a report is? A report tells facts about a topic. Facts are true things. I have a dog named Rags. That's a fact about me.

I'll show you a report I wrote about the Fourth of July. It has facts.

To the Teacher: Read the text aloud to the children. Ask children if they recognize Brad from the Expository Big Book, *Show and Tell*. Discuss how reports are different from other types of writing, e.g., stories, poetry, directions. Explain that Brad has written a report about a holiday that interests him. Read page 159.

I always use this list to write good reports.

Report Writing Checklist

☑ Tell facts. Tell *who, what, where, when, why.*

☑ Start with a good topic sentence.
End with a good closing sentence.

☑ Start each sentence with a capital letter.

☑ End each sentence with **.** or **?** or **!**

☑ Make sure each sentence has a doer and an action.

This is my report about the Fourth of July.

The Fourth of July
by Brad

The Fourth of July is an American holiday. It's a day to celebrate America's freedom. People all over America have fun! They have cookouts. They march in parades. They watch fireworks at night. The Fourth of July is an important holiday.

To the Teacher: Invite volunteers to read all or part of Brad's report. Help children identify the facts that Brad included in his report. Then discuss the checklist questions on page 161.

Report Writing Checklist Questions

☑	Does the report tell facts? Does the report tell *who, what, where, when, why*?	yes	no
☑	Does the report start with a good topic sentence and end with a good closing sentence?	yes	no
☑	Does each sentence start with a capital letter?	yes	no
☑	Is there **.** or **?** or **!** at the end of each sentence?	yes	no
☑	Does each sentence have a doer and an action?	yes	no

Gather Ideas

Find books about my topic.

Here's how I wrote my report. First, I decided to write about the Fourth of July. That's my topic. Then I looked for books with facts about my topic. I listed the books but crossed out the third one. It didn't give facts about the Fourth of July.

Now it's your turn! Choose a holiday. Find some books that tell about it.

My Topic
Fourth of July

My Books
All About the Fourth of July
Holidays in the United States
~~The Statue of Liberty~~

To the Teacher: Read the text aloud to the children. Explain that Brad listed some books he found, and tell why he crossed out *The Statue of Liberty*. Brainstorm holidays with the children. After they have chosen a holiday and located books about it, have them complete pages 163 and 164. Guide children.

Your Own Writing
Prewriting

Name

Directions: Choose a holiday. Write it under "My Topic." Find books about your holiday. Write them down.

My Topic

My Books

Name

Directions: Write the names of other books.

My Books

To the Teacher: Remind children that the books they choose should tell facts, especially important facts, about their holiday. Three books should be enough. Read page 165 together.

164

Make a Plan

Plan my report. Take notes. Make a web.

I decided to write notes from my books in a web. I made sure to take notes only about the Fourth of July. My notes tell facts.

I enjoyed making a web! Look on the next page to see it.

Prewriting

Make a Plan

Plan my report. Take notes. Make a web.

Brad's Web

Fourth of July

- celebrates America's freedom
- fun all over America
- cookouts and parades
- fireworks at night

To the Teacher: Read this page with the children. Explain to them what a web is and why it is used. You may wish to show children the web on the back of the Expository Big Book, *Show and Tell*. Then reread Brad's report on page 160. Have children discuss how Brad's web helped him write his report. Read page 167 together.

Do you like my web? Now you can make a web. Show what you found out about your holiday.

Use the next page to get your web started. Have fun!

Your Own Writing
Prewriting

Name _____

Directions: Write the name of your holiday in the box. That is your topic.

CUT and MAKE

You will use this page to make a web.

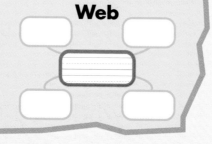

Web

My Topic

To the Teacher: Ask children to tear out pages 163 and 164. Have them write the name of their holiday in the box on page 168. Then have children add two facts to the web on page 169. Tell children that they will cut out and assemble their web later. When cutting, **make sure** children start at "Cut here." and stay on the dotted lines.

Cut here.

Your Own Writing
Prewriting

Name _____

Directions: Use the books you found. Write one fact about your holiday in each box.

✂ CUT and MAKE

You will use this page to make a web.

Web

Cut here.

Your Own Writing
Prewriting

Name _____

Directions: Use the books you found. Write one fact about your holiday in each box.

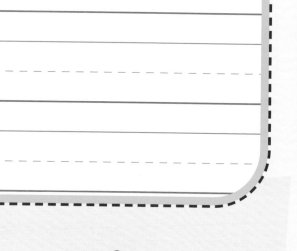

CUT and **MAKE**

You will use this page to make a web.

Web

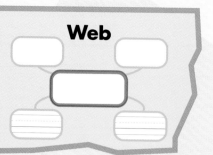

To the Teacher: Have children add facts to the boxes on this page. Then help them tear out pages 168–170, cut out the web, and paste it together onto a large, separate sheet of paper. When cutting, **make sure** children start at "Cut here." and stay on the dotted lines. Remember, pages 169 and 170 are back-to-back. Read page 171 with the children.

170

Drafting
Write
Use my web. Write a sentence for each yellow box.

Next, I wrote my draft. I put the facts from my web into sentences. I know there are rules about sentences—like the ones I learned about capital letters and punctuation.

I tried my best to follow the rules. I liked getting my ideas down.

Drafting
Write

Use my web. Write a sentence for each yellow box.

I used my web to write my report. I tried to write sentences. Read my draft on the next page.

Brad's Web

celebrates America's freedom

fun all over America

Fourth of July

cookouts and parades

fireworks at night

To the Teacher: Read the text aloud to the children. Then read page 173. Discuss how Brad used the facts in his web to write sentences about the holiday. Note that the words in Brad's draft are underlined in yellow—the same color that surrounds the boxes from which the words came.

The Fourth of July It's a day to celebrate America's freedom. People all over America have fun! They have cookouts. They march in parades. fireworks at night.

Do you see how I used my web to write my report? Now it's your turn.

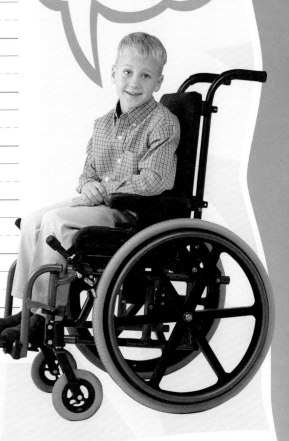

Your Own Writing
Drafting

DRAFT

Name

Directions: Pick a fact from your web. Write one sentence in the yellow box about that fact.

My Topic Sentence

A Sentence About My Holiday

To the Teacher: Read the directions with the children. Tell them they will write in the green box later. Guide children in using one yellow box from their web to write a sentence in the yellow box here. On page 175, have them write two more sentences. Children should have their web beside them. Point out the color relationship.

Name

Directions: Pick two more facts from your web. Write one sentence in each yellow box about each fact.

A Sentence About My Holiday

A Sentence About My Holiday

Your Own Writing
Drafting

DRAFT

Name _____

Directions: Pick the last fact from your web. Write one sentence in the yellow box about that fact.

A Sentence About My Holiday

My Closing Sentence

To the Teacher: Read the directions with the children. Tell them they will write in the red box later. Guide children in using the last yellow box from their web to write a sentence in the yellow box here. Read page 177 together.

Read My Paper

Use my web. Use the green and red box to write a topic sentence and a closing sentence.

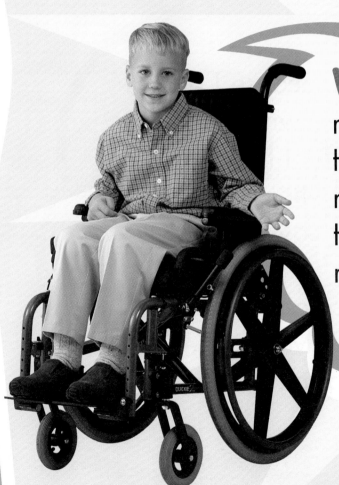

When my draft was finished, I read my paper. I noticed some things I could change to make my report even better. Look at the next two pages. You can see how I revised my report.

Revising

Read My Paper

Use my web. Use the green and red box to write a topic sentence and a closing sentence.

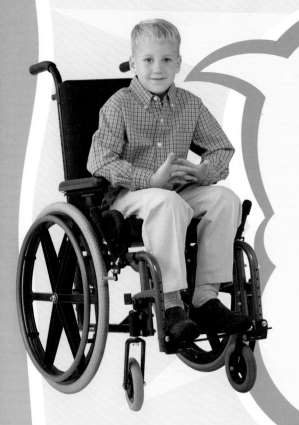

My report got better because I added some sentences. Here's what I did.

1. I added a sentence at the beginning. It tells my readers what my report is about. My teacher says that's called a "topic sentence."

2. I added a sentence at the end. It sums up my report. My teacher says that's called a "closing sentence."

To the Teacher: Read why Brad made changes. Then read Brad's revised report on page 179. Ask children to point to the sentences Brad added. Discuss whether Brad's changes improved his report and why. Remind children that both sentences use the topic from the green and red center box of his web. The topic sentence is underlined in green because it comes first, and the closing sentence is underlined in red because it comes last.

The Fourth of July
It's a day to celebrate America's freedom. People all over America have fun! They have cookouts. They march in parades. fireworks at night.

The Fourth of July is an American holiday.

The Fourth of July is an important holiday.

Your Own Writing
Revising

Directions: Tear out the report you wrote on pages 174–176. Use the steps below to check your draft.

My Revising Steps

Step 1 Read my report out loud or to myself.

Step 2 Add a topic sentence to tell what my report is about. Add a closing sentence to sum up my report.

Step 3 Read my report again. Is it better?

To the Teacher: Read the directions with the children. They will tear out pages 174–176. Have them write a topic sentence in the green box on page 174 and a closing sentence in the red box on page 176. After children revise their reports, read page 181 together.

Next, I needed to edit my report. I asked a partner for help. Think about this tip when you work with a partner.

Talk With a Partner Tip

Be nice.

Use kind words to talk about your partner's paper. Don't hurt your partner's feelings.

Proofread

Check for complete sentences.

I read my report with Brandi. Then we checked for complete sentences. Look on the next page. Do you see how I fixed my sentence to have a "doer" and an "action"?

Complete Sentences

Make sure that each sentence has a **doer** and an **action**.

The **doer** is the **subject**. It tells who did something.

The **action** is the **verb**. It tells what the subject did.

Proofreading Mark

∧

Draw a caret to show where words should be added.

A caret looks like this ∧ .

The Fourth of July

It's a day to celebrate America's freedom. People all over America have fun! They have cookouts. They march in parades. fireworks at night.

They watch

The Fourth of July is an American holiday.

The Fourth of July is an important holiday.

Your Own Writing
Editing

Directions: Read the draft you wrote on pages 174–176. Fix mistakes. Use the checklist questions on page 161, too.

Publishing

Share
Read my report aloud to a small group.

Now I was ready to make a clean copy of my report with my name on it. I made all the changes and used my best hand-writing. I drew pictures, too. Then I read it out loud to a small group of classmates. They thought it was good!

Your Own Writing
Publishing

Directions: Copy your report onto a clean sheet of paper.

To the Teacher: Read the text on pages 184 and 185. Have children publish their factual reports on separate paper or in a journal. Then help them use the checklist questions on page 161 to assess their writing. Invite children to read their reports aloud to a small group.

The Fourth of July
by Brad

The Fourth of July is an American holiday. It's a day to celebrate America's freedom. People all over America have fun! They have cookouts. They march in parades. They watch fireworks at night. The Fourth of July is an important holiday.

Report on a Hero

FACTUAL REPORT

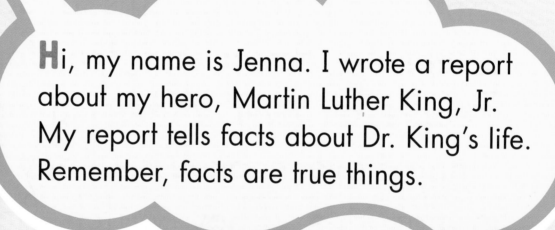

Hi, my name is Jenna. I wrote a report about my hero, Martin Luther King, Jr. My report tells facts about Dr. King's life. Remember, facts are true things.

I'm going to show you my report. I'll tell you how I wrote it, too.

To the Teacher: Read the text aloud to the children. Introduce Jenna. Discuss how reports are different from other types of writing, e.g., stories, poetry, directions. Tell children that Jenna has written a report about her hero. Discuss what a hero is by asking children, "Who is a hero? Do you have a hero?" Read page 187.

Here's a list I always use to write good reports.

Report Writing Checklist

☑ Tell facts. Tell *who, what, where, when, why.*

☑ Start with a good topic sentence.
End with a good closing sentence.

☑ Start each sentence with a capital letter.

☑ End each sentence with **.** or **?** or **!**

☑ Make sure each sentence has a doer and an action.

This is my report. It tells about Martin Luther King, Jr.

Martin Luther King, Jr.
by Jenna

Dr. Martin Luther King, Jr. is an American hero. He was born on January 15, 1929. Dr. King wanted all people to be treated the same. He worked for his dream. Now we celebrate a holiday on his birthday. Dr. King is a real hero.

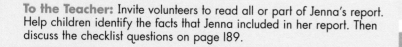

Directions: Talk about the questions. Circle **yes** or **no** to show if Jenna followed this Report Writing Checklist.

Report Writing Checklist Questions

☑	Does the report tell facts? Does the report tell *who, what, where, when, why*?	yes	no
☑	Does the report start with a good topic sentence and end with a good closing sentence?	yes	no
☑	Does each sentence start with a capital letter?	yes	no
☑	Is there **.** or **?** or **!** at the end of each sentence?	yes	no
☑	Does each sentence have a doer and an action?	yes	no

Prewriting
Gather Ideas

Find books about my topic.

For my report, I chose my topic first— Martin Luther King, Jr. He's the hero I wanted to write about. Then I looked for books with facts about my topic. I made a list but crossed out the second book. It didn't tell facts about Dr. King.

Now you can try! Pick a hero. Find some books with facts about your hero.

My Topic
Martin Luther King, Jr.

My Books
The Life of Martin Luther King, Jr.
~~King of the World~~
American Heroes

Name

Directions: Choose a hero. Write it under "My Topic." Find books about your hero. Write them down.

My Topic

My Books

Name

Directions: Write the names of other books.

My Books

To the Teacher: Remind children that the books they choose should tell facts, especially important facts, about their hero. Three books should be enough. Read page 193 together.

192

Make a Plan

Plan my report. Take notes. Make a web.

The next thing I did was write notes from my books in a web. I was careful to take notes only about Martin Luther King, Jr. My notes tell facts.

Making a web was fun! You can see my web on the next page.

Prewriting
Make a Plan

Plan my report. Take notes. Make a web.

Jenna's Web

born on
January 15, 1929

wanted all
people to be
treated the same

Martin Luther King, Jr.

worked for his
dream

birthday
a holiday

To the Teacher: Read this page with the children. Remind them what a web is and why it is used. Then reread Jenna's report on page 188. Have children discuss how Jenna's web helped her write her report. Read page 195 together.

194

What do you think of my web? Now it's your turn. Make your own web. Tell what you found out about your hero.

You can start your web on the next page. I know you can do it!

Your Own Writing
Prewriting

Name _____

Directions: Write the name of your hero in the box. That is your topic.

CUT and MAKE

You will use this page to make a web.

Web

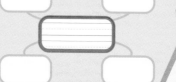

My Topic

To the Teacher: Ask children to tear out pages 191 and 192. Have them write the name of their hero in the box on page 196. Then have children add two facts to the web on page 197. Tell children that they will cut out and assemble their web later. When cutting, **make sure** children start at "Cut here." and stay on the dotted lines.

Cut here.

Name

Directions: Use the books you found. Write one fact about your hero in each box.

CUT and **MAKE**

You will use this page to make a web.

Web

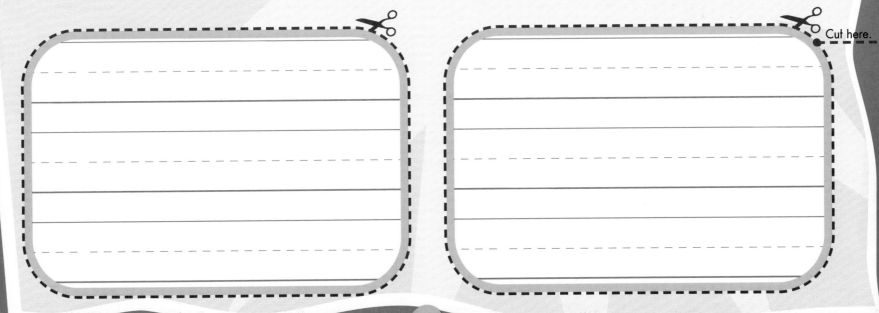

Cut here.

Your Own Writing
Prewriting

Name _____

Directions: Use the books you found. Write one fact about your hero in each box.

✂ Cut here.

CUT and MAKE

Web

You will use this page to make a web.

Drafting
Write

Use my web. Write a sentence for each yellow box.

Here's what I did next. I wrote my draft by putting the facts from my web into sentences.

I knew the most important thing was to put my ideas on paper. I could fix my mistakes later.

Drafting

Write

Use my web. Write a sentence for each yellow box.

I used my web to write my report. I tried to write sentences. The next page shows my draft.

Jenna's Web

born on January 15, 1929

wanted all people to be treated the same

Martin Luther King, Jr.

worked for his dream

birthday a holiday

Martin Luther King, Jr. on January 15, 1929. Dr. King wanted all people to be treated the same. He worked for his dream. Now we celebrate a holiday on his birthday.

Remember, I used my web to write my report. Now you can try.

Your Own Writing
Drafting

DRAFT

Name _____

Directions: Pick a fact from your web. Write one sentence in the yellow box about that fact.

My Topic Sentence

A Sentence About My Hero

To the Teacher: Read the directions with the children. Tell them they will write in the green box later. Guide children in using one yellow box from their web to write a sentence in the yellow box here. On page 203, have them write two more sentences. Children should have their web beside them. Point out the color relationship.

Your Own Writing
Drafting

DRAFT

Directions: Pick two more facts from your web. Write one sentence in each yellow box about each fact.

A Sentence About My Hero

A Sentence About My Hero

Your Own Writing
Drafting

DRAFT

Directions: Pick the last fact from your web. Write one sentence in the yellow box about that fact.

A Sentence About My Hero

My Closing Sentence

To the Teacher: Read the directions with the children. Tell them they will write in the red box later. Guide children in using the last yellow box from their web to write a sentence in the yellow box here. Read page 205 together.

204

Read My Paper

Use my web. Use the green and red box to write a topic sentence and a closing sentence.

Next, I read my paper. I thought about what I wrote. I saw places where I could make changes. The changes would make my report even better. Look at the next two pages to see how I revised my report.

Read My Paper

Use my web. Use the green and red box to write a topic sentence and a closing sentence.

I saw that I needed to add some sentences. Here's why I made changes.

1. I added a topic sentence at the beginning. It tells what my report is about.

2. I added a closing sentence at the end. It brings together all the ideas in my report.

To the Teacher: Read why Jenna made changes. Then read Jenna's revised report on page 207. Ask children to point to the sentences Jenna added. Discuss whether Jenna's changes improved her report and why. Remind children that both sentences use the topic from the green and red center box of her web. The topic sentence is underlined in green because it comes first, and the closing sentence is underlined in red because it comes last.

Martin Luther King, Jr. on January 15, 1929. Dr. King wanted all people to be treated the same. He worked for his dream. Now we celebrate a holiday on his birthday.

Dr. Martin Luther King, Jr. is an American hero.

Dr. King is a real hero.

Your Own Writing
Revising

Directions: Tear out the report you wrote on pages 202–204. Use the steps below to check your draft.

My Revising Steps

Step 1 Read my report out loud or to myself.

Step 2 Add a topic sentence to tell what my report is about. Add a closing sentence to sum up my report.

Step 3 Read my report again. Is it better?

To the Teacher: Read the directions with the children. They will tear out pages 202–204. Have them write a topic sentence in the green box on page 202 and a closing sentence in the red box on page 204. After children revise their reports, read page 209 together.

Next, I asked a partner to help me edit my report. Here's a nice tip for talking with a partner.

Talk With a Partner Tip

Be honest.

Be nice, but tell your partner what you really think. Don't pretend that everything is good just because your partner is your friend. First, find at least one thing you like. Then find one thing that could be better.

Editing

Proofread

Check for complete sentences.

I read my report with Maria. We looked for complete sentences. I used the proofreading mark to show where to put the "doer" and "action." On the next page, you can see how I fixed my mistake.

Skills

Complete Sentences

Make sure that each sentence has a **doer** and an **action**.

The **doer** is the **subject**. It tells who did something.

The **action** is the **verb**. It tells what the subject did.

Proofreading Mark

∧

Draw a caret to show where words should be added.

A caret looks like this ∧.

To the Teacher: Read the text aloud to the children. Review the skill and the proofreading mark. Ask children to look at page 211 and find the words Jenna added to her report. Then have children read their drafts and fix their mistakes.

 He was born

 DRAFT

    Martin Luther King, Jr. on January 15, 1929. Dr. King wanted all people to be treated the same. He worked for his dream. Now we celebrate a holiday on his birthday.

Dr. Martin Luther King, Jr. is an American hero.

Dr. King is a real hero.

Your Own Writing
Editing

Directions: Read the draft you wrote on pages 202–204. Fix mistakes. Use the checklist questions on page 189, too.

Publishing
Share

Publish my report in a book for the classroom library.

Then I was ready to copy my report. I made all the changes I had marked, and I wrote my name. I used my best handwriting. I made my report into a neat book for my classroom library. Then everyone could read it!

Your Own Writing
Publishing

Directions: Copy your report onto a clean sheet of paper.

Martin Luther King, Jr.

by Jenna

Dr. Martin Luther King, Jr. is an American hero. He was born on January 15, 1929. Dr. King wanted all people to be treated the same. He worked for his dream. Now we celebrate a holiday on his birthday. Dr. King is a real hero.

Your Own Writing
EXPOSITORY

Directions: Use the strategies from this unit. Write a factual report. Pick an idea below. Use this idea for your own paper. Follow the steps in the writing process. Use the checklists to check your writing.

FACTUAL REPORT

Write a report about your town, your city, or your state.

FACTUAL REPORT

Write a report about an invention that helps us do things.

portfolio

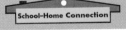
School–Home Connection

Keep a writing folder. Take your writing folder home to share.

PERSUASIVE

Writing to Tell What I Think

1

My Favorite Game

2

My Favorite Book

Theme: My World

My Favorite Game

Hi, I'm Tish. I wrote a paper to tell why I like soccer. My paper gives lots of reasons. Read it! Maybe you'll like soccer, too!

To the Teacher: Read the text aloud to the children. Ask children if they recognize Tish from the Persuasive Big Book, *I Love Oranges!* Talk about when and why people might try to convince others of their opinions. Explain that Tish has written a paper telling why soccer is her favorite game. Read page 217.

This list always helps me write good papers about what I think.

Persuasive Writing Checklist

☑ Tell what I think (my opinion).

☑ Tell reasons why my reader should think this way, too.

☑ Use the word **because** to connect each reason with a detail.

☑ Start each sentence with a capital letter.

☑ End each sentence with **.** or **?** or **!**

☑ Make sure each sentence has a doer and an action.

My paper tells my opinion about soccer.

The Best Game
by Tish

Soccer is the best game. It's fun to play on a team because you make friends. You get lots of exercise because you run and kick the ball. You learn to be a good sport because sometimes you win and sometimes you lose. Try soccer. It's a terrific game!

MODEL · PERSUASIVE PAPER

Directions: Talk about the questions. Circle **yes** or **no** to show if Tish followed the Persuasive Writing Checklist.

Persuasive Writing Checklist Questions

☑	Does the paper tell what I think (my opinion)?	yes	no
☑	Does the paper tell reasons why my reader should think this way, too?	yes	no
☑	Is the word **because** used to connect each reason with a detail?	yes	no
☑	Does each sentence start with a capital letter?	yes	no
☑	Is there . or **?** or **!** at the end of each sentence?	yes	no
☑	Does each sentence have a doer and an action?	yes	no

Prewriting

Gather Ideas

Think of games I like.
Pick the one I like the best.

Now I'll tell you how I wrote my paper. First, I thought about different games. Then I drew two pictures of games I like. Look at my pictures on the next page.

To the Teacher: Read the text aloud to the children. Have children look at the pictures on page 221. Ask them to discuss the two games Tish chose and speculate why she decided on soccer as her favorite one.

Prewriting

Gather Ideas

**Think of games I like.
Pick the one I like the best.**

After I drew my pictures, I looked at them again. I thought of reasons why I like each game. In the soccer picture, I saw that I'm running. When I play soccer, I run a lot! That's one reason I like soccer the best!

I decided to write about soccer. Now it's your turn. What game would you like to write about?

To the Teacher: Read this page with the children. Then discuss games that they like, even though they may not play the games themselves. Have children draw a picture on page 223 of one game they like. Encourage children to think of reasons why they like the game. Tell them that a *reason* explains why something is a certain way.

Your Own Writing
Prewriting

Name _____

Directions: Draw a picture of a game you like.

Your Own Writing
Prewriting

Name

Directions: Draw a picture of another game you like.

Directions: Now choose the picture of the game you like the best. Circle that picture.

Make a Plan

Plan my paper. Make a spider map to tell my reasons.

Then it was time to make a plan. I made a spider map. I wrote three reasons. Each reason tells why I like soccer. Then I wrote a detail to tell more about each reason. My spider map is on the next page.

Make a Plan

Plan my paper. Make a spider map to tell my reasons.

Tish's Spider Map

friends

team

run and kick

exercise

soccer

good sport

win and lose

Name

Directions: Tear out pages 223 and 224. Write the name of the game you chose in the box below.

My Favorite Game

Cut here.

CUT and MAKE

You will use this page to make a spider map.

Spider Map

Your Own Writing
Prewriting

Directions: Look at your picture. Write a reason and a detail to tell why you like your game.

CUT and MAKE

You will use this page to make a spider map.

Spider Map

Cut here.

Reason

Cut here.

Detail

Cut here.

Name

Directions: Look at your picture. Write another reason and another detail to tell why you like your game.

Cut here.

Reason

Cut here.

Detail

Cut here.

CUT and MAKE

You will use this page to make a spider map.

Spider Map

Your Own Writing
Prewriting

Directions: Look at your picture. Write another reason and another detail to tell why you like your game.

✂ **CUT** and **MAKE**

You will use this page to make a spider map.

Spider Map

✂ Cut here.

Reason

✂ Cut here.

Detail

✂ Cut here.

To the Teacher: Have children complete the last leg of their spider map on this page. Then help them tear out pages 227–230, cut out the spider map, and paste it together onto a large, separate sheet of paper. When cutting, **make sure** children stay on the dotted lines. Read page 231 with the children.

Drafting
Write

Use my spider map to tell what I think.

The next thing I did was write my draft. I used the center of my spider map to help me write my topic sentence. Then I used the legs to help me get my other ideas down on paper. To write my closing sentences, I looked at the center of my map again.

Drafting
Write
Use my spider map to tell what I think.

Tish's Spider Map

I used the words from my spider map to write my paper. You can read my draft on the next page.

friends

team

exercise   run and kick

soccer

good sport   win and lose

To the Teacher: Read this page. Explain the relationship between Tish's spider map (or plan) and her draft. On page 233, point out the connection between the sentences that are underlined in green, yellow, orange, and red and the sections of Tish's spider map in the corresponding colors. Remind children that green represents the topic sentence and red represents the closing sentences. To review *topic sentence* and *closing sentence*, see page 178.

The Best Game

Soccer is the best game
It's fun to play on a team
you make friends. you get lots
of exercise you run and kick
the ball. learn to be a good
sport sometimes you win and
sometimes you. Try soccer.
It's a terrific game!

Remember, my spider map helped me write my paper. Now it's your turn.

Your Own Writing
Drafting

DRAFT

Directions: Write a topic sentence about your game in the green box. Then look at one leg of your spider map. Write the first reason you like your game in the yellow and orange box. Give a detail about your reason, too.

My Topic Sentence

First Reason and Detail

To the Teacher: Have children write a topic sentence in the green box. To review *topic sentence*, see page 178. Have them write one reason and a detail about why they like their game in the yellow and orange box. On page 235, have children write a second reason and a detail. Children should have their spider map beside them. Point out the color relationship between the spider map and the drafting boxes.

Your Own Writing
Drafting

DRAFT

Directions: Look at another leg of your spider map. Write the second reason you like your game. Give a detail about your reason, too.

Second Reason and Detail

Your Own Writing
Drafting

DRAFT

Directions: Look at the last leg of your spider map. Write the third reason and detail. Then write a closing sentence about your game in the red box.

Third Reason and Detail

My Closing Sentence

To the Teacher: In the yellow and orange box on this page, have children write about the third reason they like their game, including a detail. Ask them to write a closing sentence in the red box. To review *closing sentence*, see page 178. Read page 237 together.

236

Read My Paper

Use the word "because" to connect each reason with a detail.

The next thing I did was read my paper. I had reasons and details, but they weren't connected. So I fixed that! The changes made my paper even better. The next two pages show what I did.

Read My Paper

Use the word "because" to connect each reason with a detail.

I added the word "because" three times to connect my reasons with my details.

1. I added "because" to tell why it's fun to play on a soccer team.
2. I added "because" to tell why soccer helps you get exercise.
3. I added "because" to tell why soccer helps you learn to be a good sport.

To the Teacher: Read why Tish made changes. Then read Tish's revised paper on page 239. Ask children to point out what Tish added. Discuss whether Tish's changes improved her paper and why. Is there anything else she needs to do?

DRAFT

The Best Game

Soccer is the best game
It's fun to play on a team ∧ *because*
you make friends. you get lots
of exercise ∧ you run and kick *because*
the ball. learn to be a good
sport ∧ sometimes you win and *because*
sometimes you. Try soccer.
It's a terrific game!

Your Own Writing
Revising

Directions: Tear out the draft you wrote on pages 234–236. Use the steps below to check your draft.

My Revising Steps

Step 1 Read my paper out loud or to myself.

Step 2 Look for places where I can add the word **because** to tell why. Can I connect each reason with a detail?

Step 3 Read my paper again. Is it better?

To the Teacher: Read the directions with the children. They will tear out the drafts they wrote on pages 234–236. Have children revise their drafts. Then read page 241 together.

ORAL LANGUAGE

Talk With a Partner

COOPERATIVE LEARNING

Next, my partner helped me edit my paper. Here's an important tip to think about when you work with a partner.

Talk With a Partner Tip

Stay happy.

Your partner is trying to help you make your paper better. Even if you don't agree with your partner's ideas, stay happy.

Proofread

Check for complete sentences, capital letters, and end punctuation.

> **A**fter I read my paper with Sam, we checked to make sure all the sentences were complete. Some were not, so I fixed them. Look on the next page to see how I did it!

Complete Sentences

A **complete sentence** has a subject and a verb. It starts with a capital letter and ends with a punctuation mark.

Proofreading Marks

≡ ☉ ∧

- Draw three lines under a letter to show that it should be a capital letter.

- Draw a period inside a circle to show where the period should be added.

- Draw a caret to show where words or a question mark should be added.

To the Teacher: Read the text aloud to the children. Review the skill and the proofreading marks. Ask children to look at page 243 and find the changes Tish made to her paper. Then have children read their drafts and fix their mistakes.

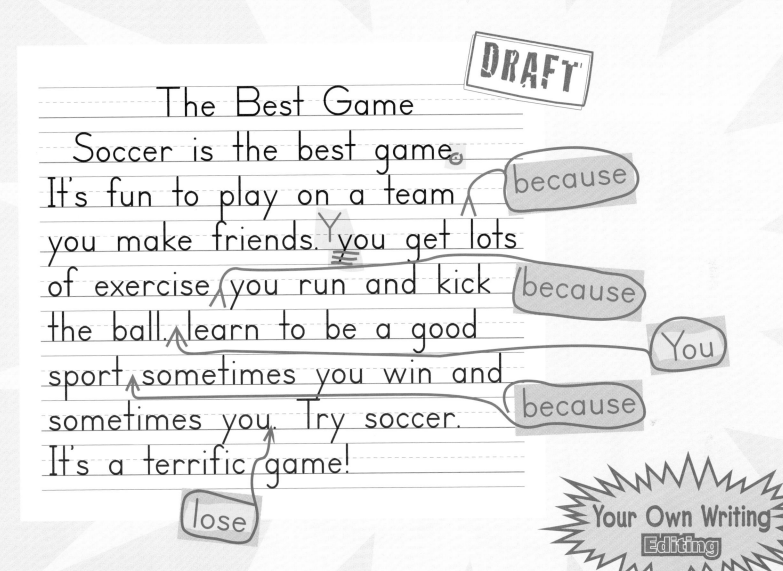

The Best Game

Soccer is the best game. It's fun to play on a team because you make friends. You get lots of exercise because you run and kick the ball. You learn to be a good sport because sometimes you win and sometimes you lose. Try soccer. It's a terrific game!

Directions: Read the draft you wrote on pages 234–236. Fix mistakes. Use the checklist questions on page 219, too.

Your Own Writing
Editing

DRAFT

Publishing

Share

Post my paper on a "What I Think" bulletin board.

When I had all my changes made, I copied my paper onto a clean sheet of paper. I used my best handwriting. I drew a new picture, too. Now my paper was ready for the bulletin board. I was glad to share it with everyone! They knew it was mine because I put my name on it.

Your Own Writing
Publishing

Directions: Copy your persuasive paper onto a clean sheet of paper.

The Best Game
by Tish

Soccer is the best game. It's fun to play on a team because you make friends. You get lots of exercise because you run and kick the ball. You learn to be a good sport because sometimes you win and sometimes you lose. Try soccer. It's a terrific game!

My Favorite Book

Hi, my name is Daniel. I wrote a paper to tell why I like the book Henny Penny. My paper gives some reasons why I think you should like Henny Penny, too. You can see my paper if you keep reading.

I always use this list to write good papers about what I think.

Persuasive Writing Checklist

☑ Tell what I think (my opinion).

☑ Tell reasons why my reader should think this way, too.

☑ Use the word **because** to connect each reason with a detail.

☑ Start each sentence with a capital letter.

☑ End each sentence with **.** or **?** or **!**

☑ Make sure each sentence has a doer and an action.

Here's my paper. It tells what I think about the book Henny Penny.

A Great Book
by Daniel

Henny Penny is my favorite book. It should be your favorite book, too. The story is funny because Henny Penny thinks the sky is falling. The story has a surprise because Foxy Loxy tricks the animals to get them into his cave. This story is exciting because Henny Penny escapes! Do you want to read Henny Penny?

To the Teacher: Invite volunteers to read all or part of Daniel's paper. Discuss with the group Daniel's reasons for liking *Henny Penny*. Then discuss the checklist questions on page 249.

Directions: Talk about the questions. Circle **yes** or **no** to show if Daniel followed the Persuasive Writing Checklist.

Persuasive Writing Checklist Questions

☑	Does the paper tell what I think (my opinion)?	yes	no
☑	Does the paper tell reasons why my reader should think this way, too?	yes	no
☑	Is the word **because** used to connect each reason with a detail?	yes	no
☑	Does each sentence start with a capital letter?	yes	no
☑	Is there . or **?** or **!** at the end of each sentence?	yes	no
☑	Does each sentence have a doer and an action?	yes	no

Prewriting

Gather Ideas

**Think of books I like.
Pick the one I like the best.**

Let's take a look at how I wrote my paper. I first thought about different books. Then I drew pictures of two books I like. You can see my pictures on the next page.

To the Teacher: Read the text aloud to the children. Have children look at the pictures on page 251. Ask them to discuss the two books Daniel chose and speculate why he decided on *Henny Penny* as his favorite one.

Prewriting

Gather Ideas

**Think of books I like.
Pick the one I like the best.**

Next, I looked at my pictures again. I thought of reasons why I like each book. In the Henny Penny picture I drew, Henny Penny looks funny staring at the sky. I like funny books! That's one reason I like Henny Penny the best.

I decided to write about Henny Penny. Now it's your turn. Which book would you like to write about?

To the Teacher: Read this page with the children. Then discuss books that they like. Have children draw a picture on page 253 of one book they like. The picture may be like a book cover and show something about the content of the book. Have children write their book title on the write-on line (accept developmental spelling). Then encourage children to think of reasons why they like the book. Tell them that a *reason* explains why something is a certain way.

Your Own Writing
Prewriting

Name

Directions: Draw a picture of a book you like.

Your Own Writing
Prewriting

Name _____

Directions: Draw a picture of another book you like.

_____
_____
_____

Directions: Now choose the picture of the book you like the best. Circle that picture.

Make a Plan

Plan my paper. Make a spider map to tell my reasons.

I knew what to do next. I needed to make a plan. So, I made a spider map with three reasons. Each reason tells why I like <u>Henny Penny</u>. Then I added one detail to tell more about each reason. Take a look at my spider map on the next page.

Prewriting

Make a Plan

Plan my paper. Make a spider map to tell my reasons.

Daniel's Spider Map

Henny Penny thinks the sky is falling.

funny

Foxy Loxy tricks the animals.

a surprise

Henny Penny

exciting

Henny Penny escapes!

To the Teacher: Read this page with the children. Remind them what a spider map is and why it is used. Point out that in his spider map, Daniel included one detail about each reason he likes *Henny Penny*. Tell children that a *detail* explains more about something. Then reread Daniel's paper on page 248. Have children discuss how Daniel's spider map helped him write his paper. Guide children in doing page 257, but remind them that they won't cut it out until later. When cutting, **make sure** children stay on the dotted lines because of the back-to-back pages.

Your Own Writing
Prewriting

Directions: Tear out pages 253 and 254. Write the name of the book you chose in the box below.

My Favorite Book

CUT and **MAKE**

You will use this page to make a spider map.

Spider Map

Cut here.

Your Own Writing
Prewriting

Directions: Look at your picture. Write a reason and a detail to tell why you like your book.

CUT and **MAKE**

You will use this page to make a spider map.

Spider Map

Cut here.

Reason

Cut here.

Detail

Cut here.

To the Teacher: Children should have torn out pages 253 and 254. Guide children to tell orally about the book they have chosen. Ask them why it is their favorite book. Make sure children wrote their book title in the box on page 257. Have them write a reason and a detail on this page. Complete page 259. Tell children that they will cut out and assemble their spider map later. When cutting, **make sure** they stay on the dotted lines.

Your Own Writing
Prewriting

Name

Directions: Look at your picture. Write another reason and another detail to tell why you like your book.

Cut here.

Reason

Cut here.

Detail

Cut here.

CUT and MAKE

You will use this page to make a spider map.

Spider Map

Your Own Writing
Prewriting

_____

_____

Name

Directions: Look at your picture. Write another reason and another detail to tell why you like your book.

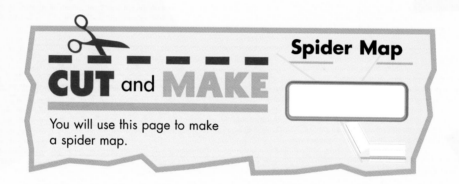

Spider Map

CUT and **MAKE**

You will use this page to make a spider map.

✂ Cut here.

Reason _____

✂ Cut here.

Detail _____

✂ Cut here.

To the Teacher: Have children complete the last leg of their spider map on this page. Then help them tear out pages 257–260, cut out the spider map, and paste it together onto a large, separate sheet of paper. When cutting, **make sure** children stay on the dotted lines. Read page 261 with the children.

260

Drafting

Write

Use my spider map to tell what I think.

Next, I wrote my draft. By looking at the center of my spider map, I was able to write my topic sentence. Then I looked at the legs to help me write my other ideas. I used the center of my map again to write my closing sentence.

Drafting
Write

Use my spider map to tell what I think.

The words in my spider map helped me write my paper. Read my draft on the next page.

Daniel's Spider Map

Henny Penny thinks the sky is falling.

funny

Foxy Loxy tricks the animals.

a surprise

Henny Penny

exciting

Henny Penny escapes!

To the Teacher: Read this page. Explain the relationship between Daniel's spider map (or plan) and his draft. On page 263, point out the connection between the sentences that are underlined in green, yellow, orange, and red and the sections of Daniel's spider map in the corresponding colors. Remind children that green represents the topic sentences and red represents the closing sentence. To review *topic sentence* and *closing sentence*, see page 178.

A Great Book

Henny Penny is my favorite book. should be your favorite book, too. The story is funny Henny Penny thinks the sky is falling. The story has a surprise Foxy loxy tricks the animals to get them into his cave. This story is exciting Henny Penny escapes! Do you to read Henny Penny

Do you see how I used my spider map to write my paper? Now you can try.

Your Own Writing
Drafting

DRAFT

Directions: Write a topic sentence about your book in the green box. Then look at one leg of your spider map. Write the first reason you like your book in the yellow and orange box. Give a detail about your reason, too.

My Topic Sentence

First Reason and Detail

To the Teacher: Have children write a topic sentence in the green box. To review *topic sentence,* see page 178. Have them write one reason and a detail about why they like their book in the yellow and orange box. On page 265, have children write a second reason and a detail. Children should have their spider map beside them. Point out the color relationship between the spider map and the drafting boxes.

Your Own Writing
Drafting

DRAFT

Directions: Look at another leg of your spider map. Write the second reason you like your book. Give a detail about your reason, too.

Second Reason and Detail

Your Own Writing
Drafting

DRAFT

Directions: Look at the last leg of your spider map. Write the third reason and detail. Then write a closing sentence about your book in the red box.

Third Reason and Detail

My Closing Sentence

Read My Paper

Use the word "because" to connect each reason with a detail.

Next, I read my paper. I had reasons and details, but they weren't connected. I saw how I could put them together, though. Then my paper would be even better. Look at the next two pages to see my changes.

Read My Paper

Use the word "because" to connect each reason with a detail.

I added the word "because" to connect my reasons with my details.

1. I used "because" to tell why the story is funny.

2. I used "because" again to tell why the story has a surprise.

3. I used "because" once again to tell why the story is exciting!

To the Teacher: Read why Daniel made changes. Then read Daniel's revised paper on page 269. Ask children to point to what Daniel added. Discuss whether Daniel's changes improved his paper and why. Is there anything else he needs to do?

A Great Book

Henny Penny is my favorite book. should be your favorite book, too. The story is funny  because Henny Penny thinks the sky is falling. The story has a surprise because Foxy loxy tricks the animals to get them into his cave. This story is exciting because Henny Penny escapes! Do you to read Henny Penny

Your Own Writing
Revising

Directions: Tear out the draft you wrote on pages 264–266. Use the steps below to check your draft.

My Revising Steps

Step 1 Read my paper out loud or to myself.

Step 2 Look for places where I can add the word **because** to tell why. Can I connect each reason with a detail?

Step 3 Read my paper again. Is it better?

To the Teacher: Read the directions with the children. They will tear out the drafts they wrote on pages 264–266. Have children revise their drafts. Then read page 271 together.

Next, I edited my paper with the help of a partner. Here's a great tip about working with a partner.

Talk With a Partner Tip

Be a good listener.

Don't interrupt. Listen to everything your partner has to say. Then you can ask questions or give ideas.

Editing

Proofread

Check for complete sentences, capital letters, and end punctuation.

I read my paper with Emily. Then we looked for complete sentences. I used the proofreading marks to show changes. Look on the next page. Can you see how I fixed my mistakes?

Complete Sentences

A **complete sentence** has a subject and a verb. It starts with a capital letter and ends with a punctuation mark.

Proofreading Marks

≡ ⊙ ∧

- Draw three lines under a letter to show that it should be a capital letter.

- Draw a period inside a circle to show where the period should be added.

- Draw a caret to show where words or a question mark should be added.

To the Teacher: Read the text aloud to the children. Review the skill and the proofreading marks. Ask children to look at page 273 and find the changes Daniel made to his paper. Then have children read their drafts and fix their mistakes.

A Great Book

Henny Penny is my favorite book. ∧It should be your favorite book, too. The story is funny ∧because Henny Penny thinks the sky is falling. The story has a surprise ∧because Foxy Loxy tricks the animals to get them into his cave. This story is exciting ∧because Henny Penny escapes! Do you ∧want to read Henny Penny?

It

because

because

because

want

Directions: Read the draft you wrote on pages 264–266. Fix mistakes. Use the checklist questions on page 249, too.

Your Own Writing
Editing

Publishing

Share **Read my paper aloud to the class.**

My last step was to make a neat copy of my paper. I made all the changes and used my best handwriting. I also put my name on it. When my paper was finished, I read it out loud to the class. They liked it!

Your Own Writing
Publishing

Directions: Copy your persuasive paper onto a clean sheet of paper.

A Great Book
by Daniel

Henny Penny is my favorite book. It should be your favorite book, too. The story is funny because Henny Penny thinks the sky is falling. The story has a surprise because Foxy Loxy tricks the animals to get them into his cave. This story is exciting because Henny Penny escapes! Do you want to read Henny Penny?

Your Own Writing

PERSUASIVE

Directions: Use the strategies from this unit. Write a persuasive paper. Pick an idea below. Use this idea for your own paper. Follow the steps in the writing process. Use the checklists to check your writing.

PERSUASIVE PAPER

Write about food you should eat to stay healthy.

PERSUASIVE PAPER

Write about some good ways to exercise.

School-Home Connection

portfolio

Keep a writing folder. Take your writing folder home to share.

Hi again! Did you like my big book? Now you'll make your own student-sized book. Then you can read it with your class!

You'll also turn my big book into a little book. Cut and fold to make a book of your own! It'll be fun! Look on the next pages.

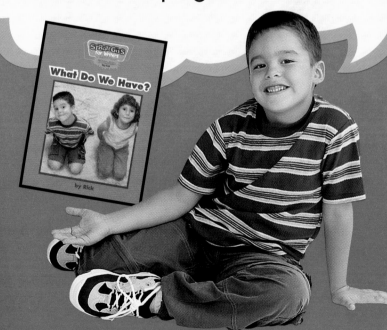

Here's my big book. You'll make a little one of this, too. Remember, when you cut, be careful and stay on the dotted lines!

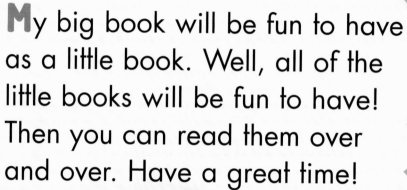

My big book will be fun to have as a little book. Well, all of the little books will be fun to have! Then you can read them over and over. Have a great time!

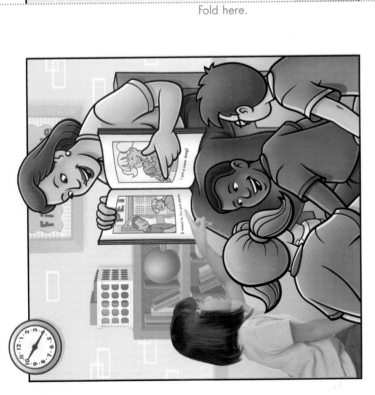

Next I read a story.

Cut here.

I went to school today.

Fold here.

I think I will come back!

Strategies for Writers

My Big Day!

Fold here.

My name is Yan.

2

Cut here.

I am in the first grade.

Fold here.

Fold here.

4

Later I made a new friend.

7

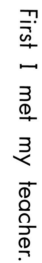

First I met my teacher.

5

Kim's toy is new and blue.

3

DESCRIPTIVE

What Do We Have?

My toy rolls.

6

Cut here.

What do we have?

A truck! A boat!

8

Cut here.

My toy is loud.

I have a new red toy.

Fold here.

Kim's toy can float.

Vrooom!

Brrrm-Brrrm!

Kim's toy is loud, too.

Fold here.

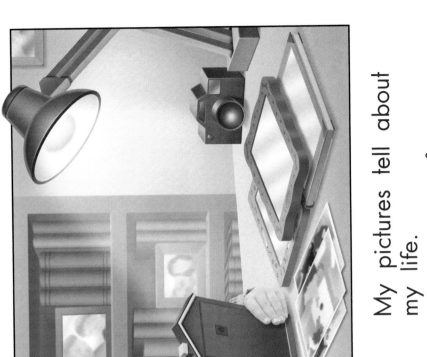

My pictures tell about my life.

3

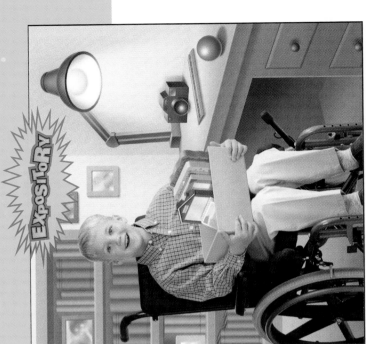

Show and Tell

I have a dog named Rags. She can catch a ball!

6

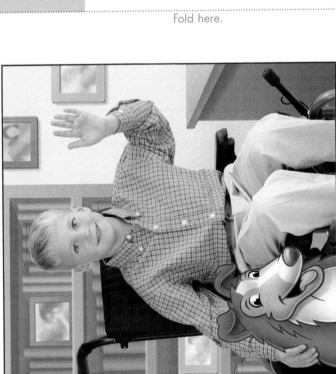

And my name is Brad.

Strategies for Writers

Let me show you my pictures.

2

Cut here.

This is my mom and dad. I help them run our store.

4

Fold here.

I go to Pine School. My teacher's name is Mr. Reed.

7

We live in this house. My room is in the front.

5

Fold here.

Oranges are so sweet and juicy.

3

PERSUASIVE

I Love Oranges!

I love oranges because they have seeds.

6

Cut here.

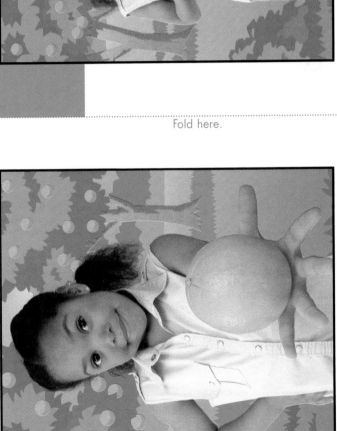

Eat an orange! I think you will like it.

8

Strategies for Writers

I love oranges because they smell and taste good!

2

Cut here.

I love oranges because they are never boring.

4

Fold here.

I can plant the seeds and grow an orange tree!

7

You can eat them lots of different ways.

5

Fold here.